CAN'T I JUST...

Educational Series

Volume One

The Career & College Collection

Originality Statement

This book is an original work written by the author and reflects their unique ideas, voice, and instructional approach. While it may reference common educational and career-planning concepts, all content, including structure, language, exercises, and framework, is the author's own creation. Any similarities to other published works are purely coincidental.

Printed in the United States of America

ISBN: 978-1-968756-94-9

First Edition

Cover design by Rachel Bostwick

Interior design and layout by Rachel Bostwick

See page 307 for your
FREE EDUCATOR TOOLKIT

TABLE OF CONTENTS

-PART THREE-
CAN'T I JUST HELP MY KID PICK A PATH?
A Career + College Survival Guide
for Parents Who Want to Get It Right

-PART ONE-
CAN'T I JUST STAY IN MY ROOM?
A Career Guide for Everyone Who'd Rather Not Talk About It

Jennifer Larsen

Originality Statement

This book is an original work written by the author and reflects their unique ideas, voice, and instructional approach. While it may reference common educational and career-planning concepts, all content, including structure, language, exercises, and framework, is the author's own creation. Any similarities to other published works are purely coincidental.

Printed in the United States of America

First Edition

Cover design by Rachel Bostwick

Interior design and layout by Rachel Bostwick

Contents

📖 Introduction:
Finding Your Path—
Without Wasting Time or Money

◆ The Big Question: What Do You Want to Do with Your Life?

At some point, everyone gets asked:

"What do you want to do with your life?"

It sounds simple, but for most people, it's **overwhelming.** Whether you're just starting out or trying to figure things out for the **fifth time**, the pressure to **"get it right"** can feel huge.

And it's not just you—**parents struggle with this too.** They want the best for their kids, and when they don't know what to say, they often **default to pushing financial security.** It's understandable—nobody wants their child to struggle. But this has led to a frustrating trend:

◆ The Two Biggest Career Pitfalls:

✕ Some students pick a degree they enjoy but **have no idea how to turn it into a career.**

✕ Others choose a major **just because it pays well**, even if they **hate the work.**

Neither path leads to happiness. **No one should spend 50 years in a job they can't stand.** And no one should go **$100,000 into debt** for a degree they can't apply.

☑ The good news? There's a better way.

◆ You Don't Have to Have It All Figured Out Yet

Many people believe that they need to **know exactly what they want to do before making any decisions.**

🚫 Wrong.

✓ **College is part of the journey, not the final destination.** You can use those years to **explore interests and build skills** instead of feeling pressured to choose the perfect major right away.

✓ **College isn't the only option.** Some of the highest-paying and most in-demand careers **don't require a degree at all.**

✓ **Your first career decision isn't permanent.** Most people **change paths multiple times** as they discover what truly fits.

This book isn't here to tell you, **"Pick a major and stick with it forever."** Instead, it will show you **how to make informed decisions, test out careers, and adjust your path as you go.**

☑ **Key Takeaway:** You don't have to know **everything** today—you just need to **start moving forward.**

◆ A Career That Actually Fits You—Not Just a "Safe" Option

This book will help you figure out a **career path that makes sense for you**—not just something that **pays the bills**, and not just something you **enjoy for fun**, but a **real, sustainable future that balances both.**

To do that, you only need to focus on **three things:**

1. **What are you good at?** (Even the skills you don't realize matter.)

2. **What do you like?** (Because passion does count.)

3. **What does society need?** (A job has to be sustainable, too.)

When you combine these three, you'll start seeing real options— careers that fit **who you are, what you enjoy, and what will actually support you.**

And once you have that foundation, making decisions about **college, trade school, bootcamps, military service, or job choices** becomes **much easier.**

◆ **College: A Good Option—But Not the Only One**

For years, people were told that **college was the only path to success.**

🚫 **That's simply not true.**

✓ Some of the most in-demand careers don't require a degree.

✓ You can build marketable skills through trade schools, bootcamps, self-teaching, or apprenticeships.

✓ If you do choose college, you don't have to pick a major right away, and you can adjust as you go.

If you're unsure about college, **this book will help you explore all of your options.**

◆ The Reality: Your Career Will Evolve—And That's Okay

Another **huge myth** about career planning is that you need to **figure it all out now** and stick with it for life.

✓ **Most people change careers multiple times.**

✓ **Industries shift, technology evolves, and new jobs appear all the time.**

✓ **The "perfect" career today might not even exist in 10 years.**

That's why this book **doesn't just help you choose a career—it also prepares you for change.**

If you **realize you want to switch paths later,** there are ways to do it **without starting over from scratch.** If the **job market changes,** you'll know how to **adapt and keep your career moving forward.**

Key Takeaway: Your first career choice **isn't your final one.** The most valuable skill you can develop is **learning how to navigate change.**

◆ **What You'll Learn in This Book**

This isn't a long, complicated book full of **fluff and outdated career advice.** It's a **straight-to-the-point guide** to help you **find direction and move forward with confidence.**

◆ **By the end, you'll know how to:**

✓ **Identify your real skills** (including the ones you don't even realize are valuable).

✓ **Uncover what you actually enjoy doing**—beyond just hobbies.

✓ **Research the job market** so you don't waste time on careers that are disappearing.

✓ **Choose a college major strategically—or decide if college is even the right path.**

✓ **Explore alternatives like trade school, bootcamps, the military, or entrepreneurship.**

✓ **Test out careers before committing** (so you don't waste years on something you'll regret).

✓ **Make a career plan—but also pivot if you ever change your mind.**

✓ **Future-proof your career** so you always stay ahead of industry shifts.

◆ **And most importantly:**

✓ **Take action.** Because all the career advice in the world means nothing if you don't apply it.

By the end, **you'll have a plan.** You won't be guessing. You won't feel lost. **And if you still need help, you'll know exactly where to find it.**

◆ **What Happens Next?**

✓ If you're **stressed about choosing a career,** this book will help you break it down into **simple, manageable steps.**

✓ If you **already have a career plan,** this book will show you how to **test it before committing.**

✓ If you're **afraid of picking the wrong path,** this book will teach you how to **pivot later if needed.**

Your **career is yours to shape.** Let's get started. 🚀

📖 Chapter 1:
What Are You Good At?

Skills Aren't Always Obvious

Most people think of skills in big, obvious ways—math, writing, sports, science. But the skills that truly shape careers often go unnoticed.

Think about it:

- ✔ Some people can sit in front of a computer for hours without getting distracted. That's a skill.

- ✔ Some are great at organizing, keeping everything in order effortlessly.

- ✔ Some instinctively know which colors match or how to arrange a space to make it feel balanced.

These don't sound like job qualifications, but they absolutely are. **The problem is, most people don't realize their own strengths because no one ever points them out.**

◆ **Breaking Past the Obvious Skills**

When someone asks, **"What are you good at?"** the typical responses are:

> ✗ "I don't know."

> ✗ "I guess I'm okay at math."

> ✗ "I like video games, but that's not a skill."

But let's dig deeper. Here are some hidden skills that people often overlook:

☑ Do you remember details well (like dates, facts, or instructions)?
  → That's a skill.

☑ Do you pick up on other people's moods easily?
  → Emotional intelligence is a skill.

☑ Do you enjoy solving puzzles, fixing things, or figuring out how something works?
  → Critical thinking is a skill.

☑ Do you find it easy to explain things to others?
  → That's a teaching or communication skill.

- **The Difference Between Skills and Talents**

A skill is something you can **learn and improve** over time.

A talent is something you're naturally inclined to be good at.

For example:

• **Skill:** You learn how to code by practicing.

• **Talent:** You naturally understand patterns and logic, making it easier for you to grasp coding concepts quickly.

Why does this matter? **Because even if you don't feel naturally talented in something, skills can always be developed.**

Example:

Let's say you're not great at public speaking. That doesn't mean you're doomed to struggle with communication forever. If you practice, take a course, and gain experience, you can **develop that skill** and become excellent at it—even if it never felt "natural" to you.

Key Takeaway: If you assume you're only allowed to pursue careers based on natural talent, you'll **severely limit your options**.

◆ **Expanding Your View of Skills**

Sometimes, the skills that seem small actually open **huge career opportunities**.

✓ **Example 1: The "Social Butterfly" Skill**

- You might think, "I just like talking to people."

- But this skill applies to careers like **sales, public relations, customer service, HR, coaching, or event planning.**

✓ **Example 2: The "Always Fixing Things" Skill**

- If you're always fixing things around the house or tinkering with gadgets, that's a **problem-solving skill.**

- This can lead to careers in **engineering, IT, mechanics, cybersecurity, or even entrepreneurship.**

✓ **Example 3: The "Creative Organizer" Skill**

- If you love organizing but also enjoy aesthetics, you might be great at **event planning, interior design, project management, or even social media marketing.**

◆ **Why Your "Weird" Skills Matter**

Think of skills as puzzle pieces. Even the small, quirky ones fit somewhere. You just need to figure out how they connect.

◆ **Example:** A person who loves video games might assume that's useless in the job world. But if they break it down into skills, they might realize:

- **Strategic thinking** → Great for **marketing, business analysis, or management**.

- **Hand-eye coordination** → Useful in **surgery, robotics, and animation**.

- **Fast decision-making** → Needed in **law enforcement, finance, and emergency response careers**.

☑ **Key Takeaway:** Just because a skill doesn't sound job-related doesn't mean it can't be turned into a career advantage.

◆ **End-of-Chapter Exercise: Discovering Your Skills**

Most people underestimate their skills—not because they don't have any, but because they've never taken the time to notice them. This exercise will help you identify your hidden strengths, track your progress, and open your eyes to career possibilities you may not have considered before.

Step 1: Start Your Skill Diary

Find a notebook, a notes app on your phone, or a document where you'll keep an ongoing list of things you're good at. This list will grow over time, helping you see your skills evolve and opening up new career ideas down the road.

◆ **Write down at least 15 things you're good at.** Don't just think of big academic skills—add things like organizing, problem-solving, remembering small details, or even knowing how to keep a group conversation going. If something comes naturally to you, it counts.

◆ **Example List:**

- ✔ Explaining things clearly
- ✔ Staying focused on tasks for long periods
- ✔ Noticing when people feel uncomfortable
- ✔ Fixing things when they break
- ✔ Finding the best deals when shopping
- ✔ Writing emails or texts that sound professional
- ✔ Planning vacations or outings
- ✔ Memorizing lyrics, scripts, or information quickly

Step 2: Find Your Hidden Skills

Answer these questions to dig deeper into your strengths:

1. **What are three things people ask you for help with?**
   (This could be schoolwork, advice, fixing things, planning events, etc.)

2. **What's something you do without thinking that others struggle with?**
   (Are you naturally organized? Do you pick up new skills fast?)

3. **When was the last time you figured something out faster than most people?**
   (Maybe you solved a problem, navigated a new situation, or learned something quickly.)

Action Step: Write down your answers in your Skill Diary—these might be skills you hadn't considered before!

Step 3: Career Connection

Now, take **three** of the skills from your list and think of at least **one career** that might use them. If you're stuck, try searching online for careers related to those skills.

📌 **Example:**

✔ **Skill:** You're great at organizing schedules.

- o **Possible Careers:** Event planner, logistics manager, executive assistant.

✔ **Skill:** You love helping friends with advice.

- o **Possible Careers:** Therapist, human resources, life coach.

✔ **Skill:** You notice when colors don't match.

- o **Possible Careers:** Interior designer, graphic designer, fashion stylist.

Step 4: Keep Adding to Your List

Your skills will evolve. What you're good at today isn't the full picture of what you'll be good at in the future.

◆ Every few weeks, **add something new** to your Skill Diary. Maybe you've gotten better at public speaking, teamwork, or learning new technology.

◆ If you ever consider a career change, look back at your list. **You might see new opportunities you hadn't thought of before.**

◆ **What's Next?**

Now that you've identified your skills—**both obvious and hidden**—the next step is figuring out **what you actually enjoy doing.**

In **Chapter 2**, we'll explore your **interests and passions** and how they can shape your career choices. Even if you're good at something, it doesn't mean you love doing it—so let's find the balance.

📖 Chapter 2:
What Do You Like?

◆ Why Interests Matter

Being good at something is valuable—but enjoying what you do is just as important.

A lot of people fall into careers simply because they have the skills for them. But if you spend 40+ hours a week doing something you don't enjoy, even a high-paying job can feel miserable.

That's why interests matter when choosing a career. If you like what you do, you'll:

✔ Be more motivated to improve.

✔ Stick with it long enough to build expertise.

✔ Enjoy your daily life instead of just counting down to weekends.

◆ The Reality of Job Satisfaction

Studies have shown that people who feel connected to their work—those who **genuinely enjoy what they do**—report higher overall happiness, productivity, and even better health. On the other hand, **those who work only for a paycheck** often experience burnout, stress, and dissatisfaction.

◆ **Example:** Two people might have the same job, but their experience can be completely different:

✔ **Person A:** Loves problem-solving and enjoys being a data analyst. They find satisfaction in uncovering insights.

✘ **Person B:** Took a data analyst job because it pays well but finds the work tedious. They constantly think about quitting.

This difference comes down to **interest and engagement.**

☑ Key Takeaway: You don't need to be *obsessed* with your job, but **liking what you do makes a huge difference in long-term success and happiness.**

◆ Interests Are More Than Just Hobbies

When people think of "interests," they often limit themselves to hobbies: drawing, playing video games, reading, or working out.

But interests go deeper than that. Think about:

☑ **Environments**: Do you like working in a busy, fast-paced setting or a quiet, structured one?

☑ **Interactions**: Do you enjoy collaborating with people or prefer working independently?

☑ **Tasks**: Are you drawn to creative projects, analytical problem-solving, or hands-on activities?

☑ **Topics**: What subjects do you find yourself reading about or researching for fun?

➤ **Example:** Someone who loves fitness doesn't necessarily need to be a personal trainer. Their interest in **health and wellness** could lead to careers in nutrition, physical therapy, medical research, or even fitness marketing.

☑ **Key Takeaway:** Your interests are more than just "fun activities." They reflect the kind of work you'll enjoy long-term.

- ◆ **Connecting Your Interests to Careers**

Some people assume that only **"practical" interests** matter in career planning. But some of the most unexpected interests can turn into careers.

- ✔ **Interest: Psychology & People Behavior** → Possible Careers: Marketing, counseling, human resources, coaching

- ✔ **Interest: Gaming & Strategy** → Possible Careers: UX design, cybersecurity, business strategy, data analysis

- ✔ **Interest: Art & Aesthetics** → Possible Careers: Graphic design, architecture, fashion, photography

- ✔ **Interest: Storytelling & Writing** → Possible Careers: Journalism, content creation, advertising, screenwriting

◆ **Example:** Think about social media influencers. Ten years ago, being a "content creator" wasn't a career path. Now, entire industries exist around video editing, digital branding, and online marketing.

☑ **Key Takeaway:** No interest is "too weird" to be useful—it's all about how you apply it.

- ◆ **End-of-Chapter Exercises: Discovering What You Love**

- ● **Step 1: The Interest Exploration Exercise**

Reflect on these five key areas to uncover interests you might not have considered.

1 **Childhood Joys** – What activities did you love as a kid? *(Sometimes, forgotten passions reveal career interests.)*

2 **Effortless Engagement** – What tasks make you lose track of time? *(These are things you naturally enjoy doing.)*

3 **Admiration** – Whose careers or achievements do you admire? *(And what about their work appeals to you?)*

4 **Volunteer Ventures** – What causes or issues are you passionate about? *(Helping others, problem-solving, creativity?)*

5 **Learning Curiosity** – What subjects or skills are you eager to learn more about? *(What do you research on your own, just for fun?)*

Action Step: Write your answers in your **Skill & Interest Diary** under a new section called **Interests**.

Step 2: The "Perfect Day" Visualization

One of the best ways to figure out what you enjoy is to **imagine a day where everything goes perfectly.**

Instructions:

- ✔ Find a quiet place, close your eyes, and picture your ideal workday.

- ✔ Think about:

  - What kind of work are you doing?

  - Where are you? (An office, a workshop, traveling, at home?)

  - Are you working with others or alone?

  - What types of tasks are you handling?

  - How does the work make you feel?

Example:

- If you imagine working outside, a traditional desk job might not be right for you.

- If you see yourself in a creative environment, a highly structured corporate role might not be the best fit.

Action Step: Write down what you imagined. Even if no clear career pops up yet, **this reveals clues about what makes you happy at work.**

● **Step 3: Interest Mapping Exercise**

This exercise helps visually connect your interests to potential career paths.

Instructions:

1 **Draw a Circle:** In the center of a blank page, write **"My Interests."**

2 **Branch Out:** Draw lines extending from the center and label each with an interest (e.g., Travel, Technology, Helping Others, Problem-Solving, Design).

3 **Sub-Branches:** Under each interest, list related activities or hobbies you enjoy.

4 **Identify Careers:** Next to each sub-branch, write careers that involve those activities.

✦ **Example:**

- **Interest:** Helping Others → Sub-branch: Teaching → Possible Careers: Teacher, Corporate Trainer, Social Worker

- **Interest:** Creativity → Sub-branch: Graphic Design → Possible Careers: Brand Designer, Web Designer, Digital Illustrator

☑ **Action Step:** Look at your **Interest Map.** Which careers show up multiple times? **Those might be strong matches for you!**

Step 4: Skill and Interest Alignment

Now, let's combine **what you're good at** with **what you like** to see where they intersect.

Instructions:

1. Look at your **Skill Diary from Chapter 1**.

2. Compare it with your **Interest Map from this chapter**.

3. Draw connections between skills and interests that match.

4. Research careers that require both those skills and interests.

Example:

✓ **Skill:** You're great at organizing schedules.

✓ **Interest:** You love event planning and social gatherings.

✓ **Career Match:** Event planner, project manager, executive assistant.

Action Step: Identify at least **three career paths** that match both your skills and interests.

◆ **What's Next?**

You now have a better idea of **what excites you and what feels meaningful.** But loving something isn't enough—**you need to find a way to turn that into a sustainable career.**

In **Chapter 3**, we'll look at what **society actually needs and what industries are growing**, so you can find a career that balances **passion, skill, and opportunity.**

📖 Chapter 3:
What Does Society Need?

◆ Why Career Demand Matters

Loving a career and having the skills for it is great—but if no one is hiring for it, or the industry is dying, it won't be sustainable.

Many people make career choices based only on what they like or what they're good at, only to find out later that:

✕ The job market is shrinking.

✕ The pay isn't enough to support their lifestyle.

✕ There's too much competition, making it hard to break in.

To build a career that actually works **long-term**, you need to ask:

☑ **Are there jobs available in this field?**

☑ **Is this industry growing or shrinking?**

☑ **What do employers look for in this career?**

◆ **The Importance of Future-Proofing Your Career**

📌 **Did you know?** Some jobs that were in high demand 10 years ago **barely exist today.** Think of video rental store clerks, travel agents, and print newspaper editors. **Technology and automation have changed entire industries**, and they will continue to do so.

✔ Example 1: AI is replacing **data entry jobs, telemarketing, and even some legal research roles.**

✔ Example 2: Retail workers are being replaced by **self-checkout machines and online shopping.**

✔ Example 3: Automation in trucking and delivery may replace **millions of driving jobs** in the future.

✅ **Key Takeaway:** It's not enough to pick a career based on today's job market—you need to consider **what careers will still be thriving in 10–20 years.**

◆ **How to Research Career Demand**

Not all jobs offer the same level of growth, stability, and pay. Some industries are booming, while others are shrinking. Here's how to **find the right opportunities**:

🔳 **Look at Job Growth Trends**

Industries change fast. Some jobs that were in demand 10 years ago barely exist now. Others, like **AI, cybersecurity, and healthcare**, are growing rapidly.

🖼️ **Where to check job trends:**

✓ **U.S. Bureau of Labor Statistics (BLS)** – Tracks fast-growing jobs.

✓ **LinkedIn & Indeed Job Trends** – Shows hiring demand.

✓ **Industry Reports** – Look at market trends in fields that interest you.

◆ **Example:** The BLS reports that jobs in **renewable energy, cybersecurity, and data science** are among the fastest-growing fields, while **print journalism, manufacturing, and administrative jobs** are on the decline.

2 **Check Salary & Job Stability**

Some careers pay well but have high burnout (e.g., finance, law).

Others offer stability but low wages (e.g., some social services).

Some jobs require years of training before they pay off (e.g., medicine).

📌 **Example Salary Breakdown:**

 ✔ **Cybersecurity Analyst** → $100,000+ (high demand, good stability)

 ✔ **Elementary School Teacher** → $60,000 (stable but lower pay)

 ✔ **Journalist** → $45,000 (declining demand)

 ✔ **Physician** → $200,000+ (high pay, but 10+ years of training)

☑ **Action Step:** Pick **three careers** from your **Interest Map (Chapter 2)** and research:

- **Average salary in your region**

- **Job stability (Is the field growing?)**

- **Education or experience needed**

◆ **Hidden Costs of Certain Careers**

Some jobs may look good **on paper** but come with unexpected costs:

✔ **Doctors and lawyers** make six figures but often start their careers **deep in student loan debt.**

✔ **Corporate jobs** may pay well but require **long hours and high stress.**

✔ **Freelancers and entrepreneurs** have **freedom but no guaranteed paycheck.**

Key Takeaway: Look beyond salary—consider stress levels, education costs, and work-life balance before committing to a career.

3 Consider Automation & Outsourcing Risks

Technology is replacing some jobs, while others are being outsourced to lower-cost countries.

✔ **Safe Careers:** Healthcare, skilled trades, creative fields, technology development.

✘ **At-Risk Careers:** Data entry, retail, simple bookkeeping.

➤ **Example: Self-driving technology is advancing quickly**—this could impact careers in **trucking, delivery services, and even public transportation.**

☑ **Action Step:** Research if any careers on your list are **at risk of automation or outsourcing.**

♦ **The Rise of New & Unexpected Careers**

The job market isn't just shrinking in some areas—it's also **creating entirely new careers.**

✔ **Ten years ago, social media managers didn't exist. Now, every company hires them.**

✔ **The demand for virtual reality (VR) developers and AI specialists is growing rapidly.**

✔ **Green energy jobs (like solar panel installers) are booming.**

♦ **Example:** The world is shifting toward **sustainability**—meaning careers in **solar energy, electric vehicles, and environmental policy** will only grow.

☑ **Key Takeaway: The** best career **isn't just one that exists today—it's one that will still be in demand tomorrow.**

◆ **End-of-Chapter Exercise: Testing Career Viability**

⬤ **Step 1: Career Demand Check**

Take your **top three career choices** and research:

✔ Current job openings in your area.

✔ Salary expectations – Can it support your lifestyle?

✔ Growth outlook – Is demand increasing or decreasing?

✔ Skills/education required – Do you have them, or will you need training?

☑ **Write your findings in your Skill & Interest Diary.**

⬤ **Step 2: Industry Trends Research**

Pick **one career field** that interests you and answer:

✓ **What's changing in this industry?**

✓ **Are new technologies affecting it?**

✓ **Are companies hiring for this role, or is competition too high?**

☑ **Use online sources like:**

- **Google job market reports**

- **Industry news websites**

- **LinkedIn job searches**

☑ **Write a brief summary of what you learn in your Skill Diary.**

Step 3: Identifying Transferable Skills

If a career you're interested in is **shrinking**, can your skills transfer to a related field?

Example:

X If **print journalism is declining**, a writer might shift to **content marketing, copywriting, or digital media.**

X If **traditional retail jobs are disappearing**, someone with sales skills might move into **e-commerce or digital marketing.**

Action Step: Write down at least **two alternative career options** that use skills from your top choices.

◆ **What's Next?**

Now that you've explored what careers are in demand, it's time to **prioritize your skills and interests** to find the strongest career match.

In **Chapter 4**, we'll go through ranking exercises (like MoSCoW) to see **which career paths make the most sense for you.**

Chapter 4:
Choosing a College Major (Without Stressing About It)

◆ Why Picking a Major Feels So Overwhelming

If you've ever felt pressure to pick the "right" major, you're not alone.

✓ Parents, teachers, and advisors often push students toward **practical** majors.

✓ Society makes it seem like **your major determines your entire life.**

✓ Many students feel stuck between **choosing something they love** and **choosing something that pays well.**

But **here's the truth:**

- Your major is **not a life sentence.**

- College is **a place to explore, not just train for a job.**

- Many **successful people** work in fields **completely different from their degree.**

Key Takeaway: College isn't just about getting a degree—**it's about figuring out your strengths, interests, and career possibilities.**

◆ **You Don't Have to Choose a Major Immediately**

Did you know that many colleges **don't require you to declare a major right away?**

✓ Most students **spend their first year taking general education courses.**

✓ You can **explore multiple subjects** before committing.

✓ If you're undecided, **choose a broad major that gives you flexibility.**

◆ **Best Flexible Majors for Undecided Students:**

✓ **Business** – Can lead to marketing, finance, HR, entrepreneurship.

✓ **Communications** – Useful in PR, journalism, advertising, corporate training.

✓ **Psychology** – Opens doors in counseling, HR, market research, education.

✓ **Computer Science** – Leads to coding, cybersecurity, data analysis, AI.

✓ **Liberal Arts** – Great for law, writing, research, nonprofit work.

◆ **Example:**

A student who **likes science but isn't sure about med school** could start with a **biology major** and later specialize in **public health, environmental science, or biotech sales.**

☑ **Action Step:** If you're undecided, **write down three broad majors** that give you room to explore.

◆ **How College Helps You Discover Your Strengths**

Your major isn't the only thing that shapes your career.
College also gives you:

✓ **Internships** – Hands-on experience in different industries.

✓ **Clubs & Extracurriculars** – Leadership, teamwork, and networking skills.

✓ **Study Abroad** – Cultural experience and global career opportunities.

✓ **Networking** – Professors, mentors, and alumni can guide your career.

◆ **Example:**

A student who **majors in psychology** might realize they **don't want to be a therapist**, but they **love understanding human behavior**—which could lead them to **marketing, HR, or user experience (UX) research.**

☑ **Action Step:** Find **one new club, internship, or leadership opportunity that aligns with your interests.**

◆ **How to Flex Your Major into Different Careers**

Even if you pick a major, **you're not locked into one career.** Many degrees are **far more versatile than people realize.**

📌 **Examples of Flexible Degrees:**

- ✔ **English** → Marketing, journalism, PR, corporate training, UX writing

- ✔ **Psychology** → Human resources, sales, career coaching, business consulting

- ✔ **Biology** → Healthcare management, biotech sales, science communication

- ✔ **History** → Law, museum work, policy analysis, research

- ✔ **Business** → Finance, entrepreneurship, nonprofit management

📌 **Example:**

A **history major** who doesn't want to be a teacher could **work in law, government, research, or corporate strategy.**

☑ **Action Step:** Research **three career paths** that your major can lead to **outside of the obvious ones.**

◆ **If You Pick the "Wrong" Major, It's Okay**

Many students panic about **choosing the "wrong" major**—but here's why it's not a big deal:

- ✔ You can change majors. Many students do!
- ✔ You can add a minor to shift your focus.
- ✔ You can pivot after college—many careers don't require specific degrees.
- ✔ You can go to grad school in a completely different field.

◆ **Example:**

A student who **majored in art history** but later became interested in marketing **could pivot into advertising, museum PR, or brand management.**

☑ **Action Step:** If you're worried about your major, **list three ways to pivot from it if needed.**

- **Making the Most of Your Degree (Even If It's Not Perfect)**

Even if you don't love your major, **you can still set yourself up for a great career.**

✔ **Get real-world experience** – Internships, freelance work, or side projects can make your resume stand out.

✔ **Learn in-demand skills** – If your major doesn't teach skills like coding, project management, or social media marketing, take **free online courses** to supplement it.

✔ **Network with professionals** – Your **professors, classmates, and alumni connections** can open doors you never expected.

Example:

A journalism major who realizes **they don't want to be a reporter** could **build skills in copywriting or content marketing** and work in **corporate branding instead.**

Action Step: Identify **one skill you can develop outside your major** to increase job opportunities.

◆ **Final Thought: College is Part of the Journey, Not the Destination**

You don't have to have everything **figured out today.**

✔ Your **major is just one piece** of your career puzzle.

✔ College is about **learning, growing, and making connections.**

✔ **The real goal isn't just a degree—it's building a foundation for future success.**

☑ **Key Takeaway:** Your major **matters less** than how you **use it.**

◆ **End-of-Chapter Exercise: Making Smart College Choices**

⬤ **Step 1: List Three Flexible Majors**

✔ Identify **three broad majors** that give you room to explore.

⬤ **Step 2: Research Career Options for Your Major**

✔ Find three careers related to your major outside of the obvious choices.

⬤ **Step 3: Identify One Career-Building Opportunity**

✔ Find **one club, internship, or side project** that can help you gain skills beyond your degree.

☑ **Write your answers in your Skill & Interest Diary!**

◆ **Summary of This Chapter:**

✔ You don't have to pick a major immediately.

✔ College is about exploration—internships, networking, and skill-building matter more.

✔ Most majors are flexible and can lead to multiple career paths.

✔ If you pick the "wrong" major, there are always ways to pivot.

✔ Your major matters less than how you use it.

Chapter 5:
What If You Don't Want to Go to College?

◆ College Isn't the Only Path to Success

For decades, we've been told that **college is the only way to get a good job**—but that's **not true.**

- ✔ Some of the most **in-demand careers** don't require a degree.
- ✔ Many people **start college without a clear plan** and end up with **debt but no direction.**
- ✔ Some jobs care **more about skills than diplomas**—and there are many ways to gain skills outside of college.

Key Takeaway: If college doesn't feel like the right fit, **you have other options**—and they can lead to just as much success.

◆ **Taking a Gap Year to Figure It Out**

If you're unsure what to do next, you don't have to **rush into a decision.** Many people take a **gap year** to:

✔ Work and gain real-world experience.

✔ Travel and explore different cultures and perspectives.

✔ Try out internships, apprenticeships, or volunteering to see what excites them.

➤ **Example:** A student who isn't sure if they want to work in **healthcare** could **volunteer at a hospital** or **shadow a medical professional** before deciding.

☑ **Action Step:** If you're considering a gap year, **write down three productive ways you could spend it** to help you explore career options.

◆ **Careers That Don't Require a College Degree**

Many **high-paying, stable careers** don't require a four-year degree. Instead, they focus on **skills, training, and certifications.**

◆ **Examples of Great Careers Without a Degree:**

- ✔ **Skilled Trades:** Electrician, Plumber, HVAC Technician, Carpenter

- ✔ **Technology:** Cybersecurity Analyst, Web Developer, IT Support Specialist

- ✔ **Healthcare:** EMT, Dental Hygienist, Medical Coding Specialist, Pharmacy Technician

- ✔ **Creative Careers:** Graphic Designer, Photographer, Video Editor, UX Designer

- ✔ **Business & Marketing:** Real Estate Agent, Sales Representative, Digital Marketing Specialist

◆ **Example:** A student who loves **technology but doesn't want to go to college** could take a **cybersecurity bootcamp** and land a job in IT security.

▣ **Action Step:** Research **three non-degree careers** that interest you and list what skills or certifications they require.

◆ **How to Build Skills Without College**

Some careers require **certifications, trade schools, or bootcamps**, while others value **self-taught skills and portfolios.**

1 Self-Taught & Portfolio-Based Careers

Some industries **care more about skill demonstration** than degrees.

- ✔ **Tech Careers:** Web Development, UX/UI Design, Data Science
- ✔ **Creative Fields:** Graphic Design, Video Editing, Photography
- ✔ **Writing & Marketing:** Copywriting, Content Creation, Social Media Management

How to Get Started Without a Degree:

- ✦ Take free or low-cost courses (**Coursera, Udemy, LinkedIn Learning**).
- ✦ Build a **portfolio** with personal projects or freelance work.
- ✦ Gain experience through **internships, volunteering, or side gigs.**

- ✦ **Example:** Someone who wants to be a **graphic designer** could **teach themselves Adobe Illustrator, create a portfolio, and freelance on Fiverr or Upwork.**

- ☑ **Action Step:** Choose **one skill-based career** and list **three ways to start learning it without college.**

2 Trade Schools & Apprenticeships

Trade schools provide **specialized training** for **high-paying, hands-on careers.**

- ✔ **Shorter than college** (often 6 months to 2 years).
- ✔ **Lower cost** than a four-year degree.
- ✔ **High demand** for skilled tradespeople.

✦ **Popular Trade School Careers:**

- ✔ Welding

- ✔ Electrician

- ✔ HVAC Technician

- ✔ Auto Mechanic

- ✔ Commercial Truck Driving

✦ **Example:** An **HVAC technician** can earn **$60K+ per year** after completing a **1-year trade school program.**

☑ **Action Step:** Research **one trade school career** and write down what training it requires.

3 Bootcamps & Short-Term Training Programs

Some careers offer **fast-track training programs** to get you job-ready in **a few months.**

✦ **Examples of Bootcamp Careers:**

- ✔ **Coding & Tech:** Software Development, Cybersecurity, Data Analytics

- ✔ **Healthcare:** EMT Certification, Phlebotomy, Medical Billing & Coding

- ✔ **Business & Marketing:** Digital Marketing, UX/UI Design, Project Management

📌 **Example:** A coding bootcamp graduate can **land an entry-level job as a web developer** in as little as **4–6 months.**

✅ **Action Step:** Find **one bootcamp program** in a field that interests you and look at its job placement rates.

🔢 Military Careers & Benefits

The military offers **job training, education benefits, and career stability.**

- ✔ Paid training in over 150 career fields.
- ✔ GI Bill covers college tuition later if you change your mind.
- ✔ Hands-on experience in leadership, tech, healthcare, and aviation.

📌 **Example:** Someone who **isn't sure what career they want** but is interested in IT could **join the Air Force or Army in a cybersecurity role** and gain valuable job experience.

✅ **Action Step:** If military service interests you, **research at least two career paths within the military.**

◆ **Entrepreneurship: Starting Your Own Path**

Some people **don't want to work for someone else**—they'd rather **start their own business.**

◆ **Examples of Entrepreneurial Careers:**

✔ Freelance Graphic Designer

✔ Social Media Consultant

✔ Personal Trainer

✔ Etsy Shop Owner

✔ YouTuber or Podcaster

How to Get Started Without a Degree:

◆ Learn business basics (marketing, pricing, client management).

◆ Offer services on **freelance platforms** (Fiverr, Upwork).

◆ Test the waters **while working another job.**

◆ **Example:** A personal trainer could **get certified online, start training clients on the side, and eventually open their own gym.**

☑ **Action Step:** Brainstorm **one service or product** you could offer as an entrepreneur.

◆ **Final Thought: Success Has Many Paths**

Whether you go to **college, trade school, bootcamp, or straight into the workforce**, you can still **build a successful career.**

✔ College is one option—not the only option.

✔ What matters is gaining skills, experience, and adaptability.

✔ You can create your own path based on what works for YOU.

☑ **Key Takeaway: Success isn't about the path you take—it's about what you do with it.**

◆ **End-of-Chapter Exercise: Exploring Non-College Paths**

● **Step 1: Research Three Non-Degree Careers**

✔ Find three careers that don't require a college degree and list their training requirements.

● **Step 2: Identify One Skill to Learn**

✔ Choose **one high-demand skill** you can start learning through self-study, bootcamps, or apprenticeships.

● **Step 3: Explore One Alternative Career Path**

✔ Research **one option** (gap year, trade school, bootcamp, military, or entrepreneurship) and write down the first step to explore it.

☑ **Write your answers in your Skill & Interest Diary!**

◆ **Summary of This Chapter:**

✔ College isn't the only path to success.

✔ Gap years can help you explore career options before committing.

✔ Many careers don't require a degree but do require skills and training.

✔ Trade schools, bootcamps, military service, and entrepreneurship are great alternatives.

✔ The key to success is gaining skills and experience—no matter how you do it.

◆ **What's Next?**

You now know that **college isn't the only path to success**—but regardless of which path you take, you still need to **prioritize your skills and interests to make the best career choice.**

In **Chapter 6**, we'll go through **how to rank your strengths, interests, and priorities** so you can focus on careers that fit your long-term goals.

📖 Chapter 6: Prioritizing Your Strengths and Interests

◆ Not Everything Can Be a Priority

By now, you've identified:

✔ What you're good at (Chapter 1)

✔ What you like doing (Chapter 2)

✔ What society needs and will pay for (Chapter 3)

Now comes the tough part: **prioritizing.**

Not all strengths and interests hold equal weight in career satisfaction. **Some things you love might not be practical as a full-time job.** Some skills you have might not be ones you enjoy using daily.

◆ **The Reality of Compromise in Careers**

A fulfilling career doesn't mean you get **everything you want.** It means balancing three things:

✔ **Enjoyment** – You like the work enough to stay engaged.

✔ **Competence** – You have the skills or can develop them.

✔ **Financial Stability** – The job pays enough to support your lifestyle.

◆ **Example:**

- **You love music but don't want to be a struggling artist.** Instead of performing, you might consider music production, sound engineering, or marketing for a record label.

- **You're great at math but hate sitting at a desk.** Instead of accounting, you might explore engineering, architecture, or forensic analysis.

- **You love art but need stability.** Graphic design, UI/UX design, or branding could offer creative work with job security.

☑ **Key Takeaway: The perfect career doesn't exist**—but a great career is one where **you prioritize the things that matter most to you.**

◆ **How to Prioritize Your Strengths and Interests**

A structured way to organize priorities is by using **the MoSCoW Method**.

1 **The MoSCoW Method (Must, Should, Could, Won't Have)**

The MoSCoW Method helps businesses prioritize projects. Here, we'll use it to rank your **strengths, interests, and career needs** by importance.

Instructions: Take your **top 10 skills and interests** and sort them into these categories:

☑ **Must-Have** – Skills/interests that are absolutely essential for career satisfaction.

☑ **Should-Have** – Important but not deal-breakers.

☑ **Could-Have** – Nice to have, but not necessary.

☑ **Won't-Have** – Skills/interests that don't matter as much for career happiness.

◆ **Example:**

✔ **Must-Have:** Creativity, problem-solving, working with people.

✔ **Should-Have:** Writing, leadership, flexible work hours.

✔ **Could-Have:** Travel, social media, graphic design.

✔ **Won't-Have:** Math-heavy work, public speaking, sales.

☑ **Action Step:** Rank your own **strengths and interests** using this method in your **Skill & Interest Diary.**

2 **Ranking Your Career Priorities**

Some people prioritize **salary and stability,** while others prioritize **passion and flexibility.**

Ask yourself:

- Would I rather make **more money** or have **more work-life balance?**
- Do I want a **stable job** or something that allows **more creativity?**
- How important is **working with people** versus **working independently?**

Now, rank these priorities from **1 to 5 (1 = low importance, 5 = very important):**

- ✔ High Salary 💰
- ✔ Work-Life Balance 🏖️
- ✔ Creativity 🎨
- ✔ Job Stability 📈
- ✔ Opportunities for Growth 🚀
- ✔ Helping Others 🤝
- ✔ Independence 🔍
- ✔

📌 **Example Prioritization:**

- ✔ **5 (Very Important):** Work-Life Balance, Creativity
- ✔ **4:** Job Stability, Growth
- ✔ **3:** Salary

✓ **2:** Helping Others

✓ **1 (Least Important):** Independence

Action Step: Write your rankings in your **Skill & Interest Diary** and reflect on what matters most in your career choice.

◆ **The Dealbreaker Test**

Even if a career matches your **skills and interests**, it might not be the right fit if it clashes with your **non-negotiables**.

Ask yourself:

✔ Do I mind working long hours, or do I need flexibility?

✔ Am I okay with high-pressure jobs, or do I prefer stability?

✔ Do I need a job with clear structure, or do I prefer freedom?

📌 **Example:**

- **A high-stress corporate job may pay well,** but if you hate pressure, it's not a good fit.

- **Freelancing offers flexibility,** but if you need consistent income, it may not work for you.

✅ **Action Step:** Write down at least **three dealbreakers** you have for a career.

◆ **What Happens When You Can't Have It All?**

Sometimes, there's a gap between what you want and what's realistic. When that happens, you have **three options**:

✔ **Adjust Expectations** – Maybe you love writing but can't make a living as an author yet—so you start with content marketing.

✔ **Build Toward Your Dream Job** – If your ideal job requires experience or credentials, you take stepping-stone jobs to get there.

✔ **Blend Careers** – You love teaching and technology? Maybe instructional design is a good mix. You love business and creativity? Digital marketing could fit.

◆ **Example:** Someone who wants **to travel, make money, and work independently** might look into **remote consulting, international sales, or travel blogging.**

▨ **Key Takeaway: Career satisfaction comes from balancing reality with what you value most.**

◆ **End-of-Chapter Exercise: Creating Your Career Roadmap**

Now that you've **prioritized your strengths, interests, and values**, it's time to **create a career plan based on what actually matters to you.**

⬤ **Step 1: Write Your Top 5 Career Priorities**

Look at your rankings from earlier. Choose your **five most important factors** in a job.

📌 **Example:**

- ✔ Work-life balance
- ✔ Creative freedom
- ✔ Job stability
- ✔ Opportunities for growth
- ✔ Making a difference

☑ **Write your top five in your Skill & Interest Diary.**

⬤ **Step 2: List Careers That Align With Your Priorities**

Based on what you now know about **your skills, interests, and job market trends**, list at least **three careers** that fit your priorities.

❖ Example Career Matches:

    ✔ **Top Priority: Creativity + Job Stability** → Careers: UX Designer, Marketing Strategist, Film Editor

    ✔ **Top Priority: Helping People + Growth** → Careers: Therapist, Human Resources, Health Coach

Write down your top three career matches.

● Step 3: Identify the First Steps Toward Your Top Career Choice

Even if you're not **ready to jump into a new career today,** you can start moving toward it.

    ✔ What skills do you need?

    ✔ Are there online courses or certifications available?

    ✔ Can you gain experience through internships or freelance projects?

❖ Example:

- If you want to become a **UX Designer**, you might start by **taking a free online course in UI/UX design**.

- If you want to be a **career coach**, you might **volunteer to mentor students or new professionals**.

Write down one small step you can take toward your career goal this month.

◆ What's Next?

Now that you've **narrowed down your career priorities**, it's time to put those ideas to the test. **Before you commit to a career, how do you know if it's the right fit?**

In **Chapter 7**, we'll dive into **internships, job shadowing, freelancing, and other ways to test a career** before going all in.

📖 Chapter 7: Testing the Waters

◆ Why You Should "Try Before You Buy"

You wouldn't buy a car without test-driving it first. So why commit years of your life to a career without experiencing it firsthand?

Many people jump into careers based on **assumptions**—only to realize too late that they don't actually enjoy the work. The best way to avoid that mistake? **Test the waters before committing.**

☑ **Key Takeaway: You don't have to figure everything out right away.** By gaining hands-on experience before fully committing, you can avoid wasting time, energy, and money on a career that doesn't suit you.

◆ **Ways to Test a Career Without a Full Commitment**

1 **Job Shadowing (Best for Seeing the Day-to-Day Reality)**

- ✔ Spend a **day or week following someone** in the field to see what the job is really like.

- ✔ Ask professionals in your **network, school, or LinkedIn** if you can shadow them.

- ✔ Great for careers that sound exciting but **might have hidden challenges** (e.g., long hours, paperwork-heavy roles).

◆ **Example:** You might think being a lawyer is all about dramatic courtroom arguments, but shadowing one might reveal that much of the job involves research, paperwork, and negotiations outside of court.

☑ **Action Step:** Identify **one career you'd like to shadow** and find a professional to contact.

2 **Informational Interviews (Best for Insider Knowledge)**

- ✔ A **30-minute conversation** with someone in your desired field.

- ✔ Helps you **learn about career paths, job realities, and what they wish they knew before starting.**

- ✔ Reach out via **LinkedIn, alumni networks, or professional groups.**

✦ **Example:** A nurse might tell you that while they love helping patients, they didn't expect the **long shifts, emotional toll, and high-stress environment** that comes with the job.

☑ **Action Step:** Make a list of **three professionals** to request an informational interview with.

3 Internships & Volunteering (Best for Hands-On Experience)

✔ **Internships (paid or unpaid)** give you a real feel for a job before committing.

✔ **Volunteering can provide valuable experience**, especially in nonprofits or community work.

✔ Great for exploring fields like **education, social work, healthcare, and marketing.**

✦ **Example:** A student interested in **event planning** might volunteer for a **local nonprofit or festival** to see if they enjoy organizing logistics and managing vendors.

☑ **Action Step:** Research **internship or volunteer opportunities** related to your career interests.

4 Freelancing & Side Projects (Best for Testing Independent Work)

✔ If your career idea is **skill-based** (e.g., writing, coding, design), freelancing lets you **test the market before going full-time.**

✔ Websites like **Fiverr, Upwork, and LinkedIn** help you land small jobs to gain experience and confidence.

✔ **Ideal for careers in writing, digital marketing, graphic design, and tech.**

📌 **Example:** If you think you want to be a **social media manager**, you could start by **running an Instagram or TikTok page for a small business** as a side project.

☑ **Action Step:** Take on a **small freelance project or personal project** to test your skills.

5️⃣ **Online Courses & Certifications (Best for Skill Validation)**

✔ Some careers require specific skills—**taking an online course** can help you determine if it's a good fit.

✔ Platforms like **Coursera, Udemy, and LinkedIn Learning** offer **affordable ways to explore career-related skills.**

📌 **Example:** Someone considering **coding** might take an **intro to Python course** before committing to a full coding bootcamp.

☑ **Action Step:** Find an **intro-level online course** related to a career you're considering.

◆ The Hidden Benefits of Career Testing

Even if you test a career and realize it's not for you, **you still gain valuable skills** that transfer to other careers.

◆ Example:

- A student **interning at a law office** might decide they don't want to be a lawyer but **realizes they enjoy research**—which could lead to a career in journalism or policy analysis.

- A **volunteer who teaches kids** might not want to be a teacher but **discovers a passion for coaching or training adults.**

Key Takeaway: Every experience teaches you something, even if it just **helps you rule out the wrong career.**

◆ **Overcoming Barriers to Career Testing**

Many people hesitate to **test careers** because of fear, time constraints, or financial concerns. Here's how to overcome them:

✗ **"I don't know where to start."**

☑ **Start small.** Ask for an informational interview or take a short online course.

✗ **"I don't have time."**

☑ **Many career tests (like online courses or job shadowing) require just a few hours per week.**

✗ **"I can't afford an unpaid internship."**

☑ **Look for remote, part-time, or paid internships, or volunteer in a way that fits your schedule.**

☑ **Action Step:** Identify **one barrier** holding you back and write down a solution to overcome it.

◆ **End-of-Chapter Exercise: Putting It Into Action**

⬤ **Step 1: Pick One Career to Explore**

✓ Choose **one career from your shortlist** that you want to test first.

◆ **Example:** If you're interested in UX design, your next step might be taking a **free design course** or reaching out to a UX professional for advice.

☑ **Write down the career you want to test.**

⬤ **Step 2: Choose a Testing Method**

✓ Will you **shadow someone, take an internship, do a freelance project, or interview a professional?**

◆ **Example:** If you're considering **becoming a therapist**, you might **volunteer at a crisis hotline** or interview a practicing therapist about their experiences.

☑ **Write down your chosen testing method.**

● **Step 3: Take One Action This Week**

✔ **Send an email,** apply for an internship, or start a project—just take a **small first step!**

➤ **Example Email for an Informational Interview:**

Subject: Exploring a Career in [Field] – Would Love Your Insight

Hi [Professional's Name],

I'm interested in exploring a career in [Field] and would love to hear about your experience. I know your time is valuable, so if you're open to a quick **15-30 minute call,** I'd be grateful for any insights or advice you can share.

Would you be available sometime next week? I'm happy to work around your schedule.

Thanks in advance for your time!

[Your Name]

☑ **Write down the first action you will take this week.**

◆ **What's Next?**

By now, you've learned how to **explore careers before committing**—but what happens when you're ready to take the next step?

In **Chapter 8**, we'll walk through how to **turn career exploration into a real plan**, breaking down your next moves into **manageable, step-by-step actions.**

📖 Chapter 8:
Crafting Your Career Action Plan

◆ **Turning Ideas into Action**

You've explored your **skills, identified your interests, researched career demand, prioritized what matters most, and even tested out some options.**

Now, it's time to turn your insights into a **real plan**.

A career doesn't just happen—you have to **build it step by step**. This chapter will help you **create a clear, structured plan** that outlines what you need to do next so you don't feel stuck or overwhelmed.

✅ **Key Takeaway:** A dream career is built through **small, consistent actions**, not one giant decision.

◆ **Step 1: Set Your Career Goal**

Your goal should be **specific and actionable, not vague** like "I want to be successful."

📌 **Example Goals:**

- ✔ "Get an entry-level job in [career field] within 6 months."
- ✔ "Complete a certification in [skill] by next year."
- ✔ "Land my first freelance project in [industry] within 3 months."
- ✔ "Network with 10 professionals in my industry by the end of this year."

☑ **Action Step:** Write your **career goal** in your **Skill & Interest Diary**.

- **Step 2: Do a SWOT Analysis**

A SWOT Analysis (Strengths, Weaknesses, Opportunities, Threats) is a business tool that helps identify potential **challenges and advantages**.

For your chosen career path, ask yourself:

- ✔ **Strengths (S):** What skills and experiences do I already have?

- ✔ **Weaknesses (W):** What gaps do I need to fill? (Lack of experience, education, etc.)

- ✔ **Opportunities (O):** What resources or connections can I use to my advantage?

- ✔ **Threats (T):** What obstacles could slow me down? (Competition, industry changes, etc.)

◆ **Example SWOT Analysis for an Aspiring Digital Marketer:**

- ✔ **Strengths:** Strong writing skills, creative thinker, understands social media.

- ✔ **Weaknesses:** No formal marketing experience.

- ✔ **Opportunities:** Free online courses, networking events, freelance gigs to gain experience.

- ✔ **Threats:** High competition, rapidly changing industry.

☑ Action Step: Complete a **SWOT Analysis** for your career path in your **Skill & Interest Diary.**

◆ **Step 3: Set SMART Goals**

SMART goals ensure your action plan is **clear and realistic**.

- ◆ **Specific** – Clear and focused ("I will complete an online certification in UX design").

- ◆ **Measurable** – Can track progress ("I will complete three modules per month").

- ◆ **Achievable** – Realistic ("I can spend 5 hours per week studying").

- ◆ **Relevant** – Aligns with your career path ("This certification will help me apply for UX jobs").

- ◆ **Time-Bound** – Has a deadline ("I will finish the course in 6 months").

◆ **Example SMART Goal:**

"I will complete a 6-month online coding bootcamp and build three portfolio projects so I can apply for entry-level developer jobs."

☑ **Action Step:** Write **one SMART goal** for your career plan.

- **Step 4: Build Your 6-Month Career Action Plan**

Now, break your career goal into **small, manageable steps** to make it less overwhelming.

Example Action Plan (for someone pursuing Digital Marketing):

Month 1:
- Research job descriptions & identify common skills needed.
- Take a free Google Analytics course.

Month 2:
- Start a personal blog or social media project to build experience.
- Connect with 5 professionals in the field on LinkedIn.

Month 3-4:
- Apply for internships or freelance projects.
- Take an SEO or social media marketing certification.

Month 5-6:
- Apply for at least 10 jobs per week.
- Attend an industry networking event.

Action Step: Write a **6-month career action plan** based on your chosen path.

Step 5: Track Progress & Adjust as Needed

Your plan isn't set in stone. You might find **new opportunities,** need to **gain more experience,** or shift directions slightly. That's okay!

Ask yourself each month:

✔ What progress have I made?

✔ What obstacles have I hit?

✔ What's my next small step?

Example:

- If you planned to get an internship but haven't found one, maybe you **start freelancing instead**.

- If you're struggling with job applications, you **revise your resume or improve interview skills**.

Action Step: Set a **reminder to review your progress** every month in your **Skill & Interest Diary**.

◆ **Overcoming Common Roadblocks in Career Planning**

Many people start an action plan but struggle to follow through. **Here's how to tackle common challenges:**

✖ **"I don't have enough experience."**

☑ **Solution:** Take free courses, do personal projects, or volunteer to gain skills.

✖ **"I don't have the right connections."**

☑ **Solution:** Start networking on LinkedIn, join industry groups, attend local meetups.

✖ **"I'm afraid of failing."**

☑ **Solution:** Failure is just feedback. Adjust and keep going!

☑ **Action Step:** Identify **one personal roadblock** and write **a solution** for overcoming it.

◆ **End-of-Chapter Exercise: Writing Your Action Plan**

● **Step 1: Write Down Your Career Goal**

  ✔ Make it specific, measurable, and time-bound.

● **Step 2: Complete a SWOT Analysis**

  ✔ List your strengths, weaknesses, opportunities, and threats.

● **Step 3: Break Your Goal into a 6-Month Action Plan**

  ✔ List **small, realistic steps** you can take each month.

☑ **Write your full action plan in your Skill & Interest Diary!**

◆ **What's Next?**

You now have a **clear plan**—but making a plan is only the beginning. **Taking action is where real change happens.**

In **Chapter 9**, we'll cover how to **stay accountable, overcome procrastination, and actually take action on your career goals.**

📖 Chapter 9: Taking Action

◆ Why Action Beats Overthinking

You've done the research, tested career options, and built a solid action plan. Now, it's time for the hardest part: **actually doing it.**

Many people get stuck here. They keep thinking about their plan instead of taking action. They hesitate because they're afraid of making the wrong choice, failing, or not being ready.

But here's the truth: **Nothing happens unless you take the first step.**

Key Takeaway: The **perfect** time doesn't exist. **The best time to start is now.**

◆ Step 1: Tackle the First Small Step Today

Instead of looking at the whole journey, just **focus on your first step.**

◆ Example First Steps:

- ✔ Send an email to request a job shadowing opportunity.
- ✔ Apply for an internship or freelance gig.
- ✔ Sign up for a career-related course.
- ✔ Update your resume and LinkedIn profile.
- ✔ Schedule an informational interview with a professional in your field.

Action Step: Pick **ONE small action** from your career plan and do it **TODAY.**

◆ **Step 2: Use the Eisenhower Matrix to Prioritize Tasks**

Once you've started, how do you decide what to focus on next? **Use the Eisenhower Matrix to prioritize tasks.**

Sort your tasks into four categories:

1. **Urgent & Important** – Do these first! (Applying for jobs, preparing for interviews, completing coursework.)

2. **Important but Not Urgent** – Schedule these. (Building a portfolio, networking, gaining certifications.)

3. **Urgent but Not Important** – Delegate or streamline. (Resume formatting, organizing files.)

4. **Not Urgent & Not Important** – Avoid time-wasters. (Over-researching, watching random career advice videos.)

✦ **Example:**

✔ Urgent & Important: Submit three job applications this week.

✔ Important but Not Urgent: Enroll in an online certification course.

✔ Urgent but Not Important: Update LinkedIn profile.

✔ Not Urgent & Not Important: Watching too many motivational career videos.

☑ **Action Step:** Sort your next **five career-related tasks** using the Eisenhower Matrix in your **Skill & Interest Diary.**

◆ **Step 3: Overcome Fear & Self-Doubt**

It's normal to feel nervous or unsure when starting something new. **But fear only wins if you let it stop you from trying.**

How to Get Past Fear:

✔ **Afraid of failure?** → Think of failure as learning. Every setback teaches you something useful.

✔ **Not feeling "ready"?** → No one is ever 100% ready. Start now, and improve as you go.

✔ **Worried about choosing the wrong path?** → You're never locked in. Most people switch careers multiple times.

◆ **Example:** A person who wants to start freelancing might hesitate because they don't feel "expert enough." **Solution:** Take one small project and learn from the experience.

▦ **Action Step:** Write down **one fear or doubt** you have about your career journey. Then, write down **one way to push past it.**

◆ **Step 4: Build Career Habits for Long-Term Success**

Success doesn't happen overnight—it's built through **small, consistent actions.**

Key Habits to Develop:

✔ **Daily Career Development** – Spend at least **20 minutes a day** learning, networking, or job searching.

✔ **Networking & Relationship-Building** – Reach out to **one new professional each week.**

✔ **Continuous Skill Growth** – Stay updated with **industry trends, courses, and certifications.**

◆ **Example:** Instead of waiting for job opportunities, **make a habit of applying for one job per day.**

☑ **Action Step:** Choose **one career habit** to start this week and track your progress in your **Skill & Interest Diary.**

◆ Step 5: Stay Accountable & Motivated

Taking action is easier when you **hold yourself accountable.**

Ways to Stay Accountable:

- ✔ **Find an accountability partner** – Check in weekly with a friend or mentor about your progress.

- ✔ **Use a progress tracker** – Keep a spreadsheet or journal to record completed steps.

- ✔ **Set mini-deadlines** – If your goal is to build a portfolio, set a deadline for your first project.

- ✔ **Celebrate small wins** – Reward yourself when you hit milestones.

◆ Example:

- ✔ **Goal:** Apply for 20 jobs in a month.

- ✔ **Accountability:** Track progress in a Google Sheet.

- ✔ **Reward:** Treat yourself to a nice dinner when completed.

Action Step: Choose **one accountability method** and write it down.

◆ **Handling Setbacks & Rejections**

Rejection is a normal part of career growth. Even the most successful people have faced setbacks.

📌 **Example:**

✔ **J.K. Rowling** was rejected by **12 publishers** before Harry Potter was accepted.

✔ **Walt Disney** was fired from a newspaper job for "lacking creativity."

How to Handle Setbacks:

✔ **Don't take rejection personally.** It's part of the process.

✔ **Ask for feedback.** If you get rejected after an interview, ask what you can improve.

✔ **Keep going.** The only way to fail is to **stop trying.**

✅ **Action Step:** Write down **one setback you've faced** and how you can learn from it.

◆ **End-of-Chapter Exercise: Taking the First Leap**

Step 1: Take One Action Today

✔ Choose **one small, doable task** and complete it.

Step 2: Prioritize Your Next Steps

✔ Use the **Eisenhower Matrix** to organize your next **five career-related tasks.**

Step 3: Identify & Challenge a Fear

✔ Write down **a fear or doubt** and a **strategy to overcome it.**

Step 4: Choose an Accountability Method

✔ Pick a method to **track progress and stay motivated.**

Write everything in your Skill & Interest Diary!

◆ **What's Next?**

You're ready to start **building your career,** but what if—somewhere down the line—you **change your mind?**

In **Chapter 10,** we'll explore **how to pivot careers, switch industries, or restart when your career path no longer feels right.**

📖 Chapter 10:
What if You Change Your Mind?

◆ **Your Career is a Journey, Not a Single Choice**

Many people believe that picking a career is a **one-time decision**—but that's not how it works.

The reality is:

✔ **Your interests and skills will evolve over time.**

✔ **New opportunities will appear that you can't predict today.**

✔ **The job market will change, and you'll have to adapt.**

Instead of thinking of your career as a **straight path**, think of it as a **series of opportunities, choices, and pivots**.

☑ **Key Takeaway:** Your **first job** or **first career choice** doesn't define your entire future. **You are always allowed to grow and change.**

- **Step 1: Keep Building Skills & Staying Relevant**

The best way to stay **competitive and adaptable** is to **keep learning.**

☑ **Ways to Keep Growing:**

 ✔ Take **courses and certifications** to upgrade your skills.

 ✔ Follow **industry trends** to stay ahead of changes.

 ✔ Attend **conferences, webinars, and networking events.**

 ✔ Read **books, blogs, and listen to podcasts** about your field.

➤ **Example:** If AI is changing your industry, **learn how to integrate AI into your work rather than fearing it.**

☑ **Action Step:** Identify **one skill you want to develop** in the next year and write it in your **Skill & Interest Diary.**

◆ **Step 2: Adapt When Life Changes**

Your career path won't always go as planned. Maybe you **lose interest**, the industry shifts, or life takes you in a new direction.

◆ **Examples of Career Pivots:**

✔ A **journalist** who shifts into **content marketing** because digital media is growing.

✔ A **teacher** who becomes a **corporate trainer** because they want higher pay.

✔ An **engineer** who moves into **project management** to lead bigger teams.

The key to staying adaptable is:

✔ Being **open to change** instead of resisting it.

✔ Looking at how your **skills transfer** to new roles.

✔ Keeping your **network strong** so new opportunities come your way.

▨ **Action Step:** Write down **one way your skills could transfer** to a different career if needed.

◆ **Step 3: Set Long-Term Career Checkpoints**

Instead of thinking about **one final career goal**, set **career checkpoints** to guide you.

📌 **Example Career Checkpoints (5-Year Plan):**

☑ **Year 1:** Get entry-level job, internship, or freelance work.

☑ **Year 2-3:** Gain experience, take additional courses, build expertise.

☑ **Year 4-5:** Aim for a promotion, leadership role, or career pivot.

☑ **Action Step:** Create a **5-Year Career Checkpoint Plan** and write it in your **Skill & Interest Diary.**

◆ **Step 4: Remember That Success is Personal**

Society often defines success in **money, job titles, or degrees.** But real success is **personal.**

Ask yourself:

✔ **What does success look like for me?**

✔ **What kind of work makes me feel fulfilled?**

✔ **How do I want to balance career and personal life?**

◆ **Example:**

- Some people thrive in **high-powered careers with big salaries.**

- Others prefer **flexibility and work-life balance over money.**

- Some love being **experts in their field**, while others enjoy **switching industries over time.**

Action Step: Write your **own definition of success** in your **Skill & Interest Diary.**

◆ **Step 5: Stay Open to Unexpected Opportunities**

Sometimes, the best career moves are **the ones you didn't plan for.**

📌 **Example:**

- A college student working in a **retail job** discovers they love **visual merchandising** and ends up in **fashion marketing.**
- A programmer with a **passion for storytelling** moves into **video game design.**
- A finance major realizes they prefer **helping people** and switches to **financial coaching instead of investment banking.**

☑ **Key Takeaway:** Be willing to **explore, experiment, and embrace opportunities** that come your way.

☑ **Action Step:** Write down a **career opportunity you would have never considered before—but might now.**

◆ **End-of-Chapter Exercise: Future-Proofing Your Career**

⬤ **Step 1: Choose a Skill to Develop**

> ✔ Identify **one skill** you want to improve in the next year.

Step 2: Identify Your Backup Plan

> ✔ Write down **one way your skills could transfer** if you ever needed to switch careers.

⬤ **Step 3: Create Your 5-Year Career Checkpoint Plan**

> ✔ Set **realistic career goals** for the next **5 years.**

⬤ **Step 4: Define Success on Your Own Terms**

> ✔ Write **what success means for you,** beyond just money or job titles.

☑ **Write everything in your Skill & Interest Diary!**

◆ **What's Next?**

Careers aren't **fixed paths—they evolve.** But how do you make sure that your career stays **relevant, stable, and adaptable to change?**

In **Chapter 11**, we'll talk about **future-proofing your career** so you can **stay ahead of industry shifts, develop skills that never go out of style, and always be prepared for what's next.**

📖 Chapter 11:
How to Future-Proof Your Career

◆ **The Job Market is Always Changing—Are You Ready?**

Imagine choosing a career today and realizing **it doesn't exist in 10 years.**

✔ **Many jobs that existed 20 years ago have disappeared.**

✔ **Technology is evolving faster than ever**, replacing some careers and creating brand-new ones.

✔ **Some industries boom, while others shrink**, making adaptability a crucial career skill.

Key Takeaway: The best way to build a stable, successful career is to **stay ahead of changes and keep evolving.**

◆ **Careers That Have Changed (or Disappeared!)**

◆ **Examples of Jobs That Have Shrunk:**

> ✕ Video rental store clerks

> ✕ Print newspaper journalists

> ✕ Travel agents

> ✕ Data entry specialists (AI automation is taking over)

◆ **Emerging Careers That Didn't Exist 15 Years Ago:**

> ✔ Social Media Manager

> ✔ Cybersecurity Analyst

> ✔ AI & Machine Learning Engineer

> ✔ UX/UI Designer

◆ **Example:** Someone who **worked in traditional retail** might need to **pivot into e-commerce or digital customer service.**

☑ **Action Step:** Research **one industry you're interested in** and look at **how it's evolving.**

◆ The Top Career Skills That Will Always Be in Demand

Some skills **never go out of style, no matter how industries change.**

◆ Skills That Will Keep You Valuable in Any Career:

- ✔ Critical Thinking & Problem-Solving – AI can process data, but humans solve complex problems.

- ✔ Communication & Emotional Intelligence – Businesses need leaders, negotiators, and strong communicators.

- ✔ Tech Adaptability – New tools emerge constantly. Those who can learn new software and AI tools quickly will stay ahead.

- ✔ Creativity & Innovation – The ability to think outside the box is essential in business, marketing, and technology.

◆ **Example:** A **graphic designer who learns UX/UI design** stays relevant in **digital product design.**

☑ **Action Step:** Choose **one skill from this list** and find a way to **strengthen it** (through courses, books, or hands-on projects).

- **How to Become a Lifelong Learner (and Stay Ahead of Industry Changes)**

Instead of focusing on **one specific skill**, focus on **how to learn quickly and efficiently.**

◆ **Ways to Stay Ahead in Your Industry:**

 ✔ Take **free online courses** (Coursera, Udemy, LinkedIn Learning).

 ✔ Follow **industry news and trends** (blogs, podcasts, YouTube).

 ✔ Join **professional groups or networking events.**

 ✔ Ask **mentors or colleagues** about new developments in the field.

◆ **Example:** A marketing professional who **learns SEO and data analytics** becomes more valuable than one who only knows traditional marketing.

☑ **Action Step:** Write down **one new thing you will learn** in the next **six months.**

◆ The Power of Networking: Build a Safety Net for Your Career

Your **network is your career safety net.** The more **connections** you build, the more **opportunities** you'll find.

◆ How to Build & Maintain a Strong Network:

- ✔ Stay connected with colleagues, mentors, and classmates.
- ✔ Follow industry leaders on LinkedIn and engage with their content.
- ✔ Join professional organizations related to your career field.
- ✔ Be willing to help others—networking is a two-way street.

◆ **Example:** A former teacher who wants to shift into **corporate training** can start **connecting with professionals in HR and learning development.**

Action Step: Identify **one networking opportunity** you can take this month.

- **How to Stay Employable in a Rapidly Changing Job Market**

  ✔ Keep an eye on **emerging trends** in your field.

  ✔ Be willing to **take risks and try new things.**

  ✔ Regularly **update your resume, skills, and online presence.**

📌 **Example:** A **journalist who adapts to digital media trends** (SEO, content marketing) **stays employable** in a changing industry.

✅ **Action Step:** Find a **trend in your field** and write down **one way to prepare for it.**

◆ **The 3-Year Career Check-In: Are You Still Growing?**

To **stay relevant and avoid getting stuck**, check in on your career **every three years.**

◆ **Ask Yourself:**

✔ Am I still learning and growing?

✔ Has my field changed? Am I keeping up with new trends?

✔ Am I happy in my role, or do I need a change?

◆ **Example:** If you're in an **IT role that's becoming automated**, it might be time to **learn AI-related skills or project management.**

◆ **Action Step:** Set a **calendar reminder for a career check-in** every three years.

◆ **End-of-Chapter Exercise: Planning for the Future**

⬤ **Step 1: Choose a Skill to Develop**

    ✔ Identify **one skill** you want to improve in the next year.

⬤ **Step 2: Identify a Trend in Your Industry**

    ✔ Find **one career trend** that's growing and list a way to prepare for it.

⬤ **Step 3: Take One Action to Future-Proof Your Career**

    ✔ Choose **one action** (networking, taking a course, testing a new tool) that will help you stay ahead.

☑ **Write your answers in your Skill & Interest Diary!**

◆ **Final Thought: The Future is Yours to Shape**

    ✔ Your career is a journey, not a fixed path.

    ✔ Industries will change—but you can change with them.

    ✔ The more adaptable, skilled, and connected you are, the more opportunities you'll have.

☑ **Key Takeaway: The best way to secure your future is to keep learning, growing, and staying adaptable.**

◆ **Summary of This Chapter:**

✔ The job market constantly evolves—stay ahead of it.

✔ Certain skills (problem-solving, communication, adaptability) will always be valuable.

✔ Lifelong learning keeps you competitive—embrace new skills and technologies.

✔ Networking helps you find opportunities before you need them.

✔ Checking in on your career every 3 years helps you stay on track.

◆ **Final Thought: Your Career is Yours to Shape**

This book has given you the tools to **find your career path, test it, plan for it, and take action.**

But remember:

✔ **No decision is permanent.** You can pivot and adapt.

✔ **Learning never stops**—keep growing.

✔ **You define success, not anyone else.**

You're in control of your future. Go out there and **build it.**

◆ **What's Next?**

Now you know how to **stay ahead in a changing job market, develop long-term skills, and build a strong career foundation.**

So what's left? **Taking control of your future.**

In **Chapter 12 (Conclusion),** we'll wrap everything up and leave you with a final **push to take action and shape your own career path.**

📖 Chapter 12: Conclusion (Your Future is in Your Hands)

◆ **You've Done the Hard Work—Now It's Time to Move Forward**

You started this journey with a big question:

"What should I do with my life?"

Now, you have a **roadmap** to help you figure it out.

✓ You've **identified your skills and strengths.**

✓ You've **explored what excites you.**

✓ You've **researched career demand and opportunities.**

✓ You've **learned how to pivot if you change your mind.**

✓ You've **discovered ways to future-proof your career.**

✓ You've **created a plan, tested options, and taken action.**

That means you're already **ahead of most people.**

But here's the real secret: **Your career is just getting started.**

◆ **Your Career is Not Set in Stone—And That's a Good Thing**

If there's **one thing** you take away from this book, it should be this:

Your career is a **journey, not a final destination.**

✓ **It's okay to change your mind.** What you want today may evolve in five or ten years.

✓ **It's okay to take an alternative path.** College isn't the only route to success.

✓ **It's okay to pivot when industries change.** The best careers grow with you.

✅ **Key Takeaway:** You are never "stuck." You can **always** learn, pivot, and create new opportunities for yourself.

* **Future-Proofing Your Career Starts Now**

The world **will keep evolving.** Some jobs will disappear, new careers will emerge, and industries will shift.

The best way to prepare?

✓ **Stay adaptable** – Keep learning new skills and exploring opportunities.

✓ **Build relationships** – Your network can open doors you never expected.

✓ **Think long-term** – The best careers grow and evolve with you.

◆ **Example:**

If a career in **marketing or design** shifts more toward **AI and automation**, staying **ahead of digital trends** will help you stay relevant.

▣ **Action Step:** Write down **one skill you'll focus on improving** in the next year to keep yourself future-proof.

◆ **What Happens Next? You Decide.**

This book has given you the **tools** to figure out your path.

But **what you do next is up to you.**

- **You can take small steps today**—send an email, apply for a job, start a project.

- **You can commit to growing your skills**—take a course, find a mentor, push yourself.

- **You can redefine success on your terms**—build a career that fits **YOU**, not someone else's expectations.

The **only** wrong choice? **Doing nothing.**

☑ **Action Step:** Write down **one career action you will take in the next 24 hours.**

◈ **Final Thought: Your Career is Yours to Shape**

If you ever feel lost again, **come back to this process:**

✓ Look at your **skills.**

✓ Check in with your **interests.**

✓ See what's happening in the **job market.**

✓ **Test new opportunities.**

✓ **Make a plan and take action.**

Your career is **yours to create**—one step at a time.

Now **go make it happen.**

-PART TWO-
CAN'T I JUST SKIP COLLEGE?

For Everyone Who Closed the First Book and Still Didn't Want a Dorm Room

Jennifer Larsen

Contents

📖 Introduction: Success Without College

For as long as you can remember, you've probably been told that college is **the** path to success. Teachers, parents, and society push the idea that **a degree equals a good job, stability, and a better life.** And for some people, that's true.

But what if college **isn't** the right fit for you? What if the idea of spending four (or more) years in a classroom, taking on tens of thousands of dollars in debt, doesn't sound like the best way to start your life?

Here's the truth: **College is just one path—not the only path.** There are **high-paying careers, fulfilling jobs, and entrepreneurial opportunities** that don't require a degree. And choosing to skip college now **doesn't mean you can't go later.** It just means you're taking a different approach—one that gets you earning money faster and avoids student debt while still keeping your future open.

What This Book Will Help You Do

This book is your **guide to success without a degree.** It will show you:

- **Careers that don't require college** but still pay well and have room for growth.
- **Entrepreneurial and freelancing options** if you'd rather work for yourself.
- **Alternative education paths** that don't cost a fortune.
- **How to get hired without a degree** and stand out in the job market.
- **How to build long-term career success** even without a diploma.
- **The financial advantages** of skipping or delaying college—and how to make your money work for you.

This book **isn't anti-college**—it's **pro-options.** If you ever decide you need a degree down the line (for management roles, career shifts, or personal goals), you can always pursue it **on your own terms.** But if you're looking for a way to start a **successful career now, without spending years in school,** this book will show you exactly how to do it.

🎯 **Let's get started.**

📖 Section 1:
High-Paying Careers Without a Degree

When most people think of high-paying jobs, they assume a college degree is required. But that's **not** the case. There are **plenty of well-paying careers** that don't require four years of school—many of which let you start earning money much faster than your college-bound peers.

In this section, we'll explore some of the best career options that don't require a degree, including:

- **Skilled Trades** – Jobs that build and repair the world around us
- **Tech Careers** – High-paying digital and IT jobs with certifications instead of degrees
- **Public Service & First Responders** – Stable careers with strong benefits
- **Medical Careers Without a Degree** – Essential roles in healthcare that don't require a four-year diploma
- **Manufacturing & Logistics** – High-demand jobs that keep industries running
- **High-Value Sales** – A lucrative field where **your skills matter more than your education**

Let's break down these paths and how you can get started.

Skilled Trades: Building, Fixing, and Keeping the World Running

Skilled trades are some of the most **secure, high-paying, and in-demand** careers out there. These are jobs that **can't be outsourced**—someone **has** to install electrical wiring, repair HVAC systems, or build houses **right here.**

🔧 **Examples of Skilled Trades:**

- ✔ **Electricians** ($50K–$90K+ per year)

- ✔ **Plumbers** ($50K–$100K+ per year)

- ✔ **HVAC Technicians** ($45K–$80K per year)

- ✔ **Welders & Fabricators** ($40K–$85K per year)

- ✔ **Carpenters** ($45K–$80K per year)

- ✔ **Heavy Equipment Operators** ($50K–$95K per year)

💰 **Why Choose This Path?**

- ☑ **Earn while you learn** – Many trades offer **paid apprenticeships,** meaning you get paid **while training.**

- ☑ **No student loan debt** – Trade schools cost a fraction of college tuition.

- ☑ **High demand & job security** – Trades are always needed, and demand is growing.

- ☑ **Growth potential** – Start as an apprentice, become a journeyman, and later open your own business.

🚀 How to Get Started:

✔ Look for **apprenticeship programs** in your area (often found through unions or trade schools).

✔ Consider a **trade school** (usually 6 months to 2 years).

✔ **Start as an entry-level helper** and gain hands-on experience.

Tech Careers: High-Paying Jobs Without a Degree

Tech jobs aren't just for people with computer science degrees. Many **high-paying tech careers** can be started with **certifications, bootcamps, or self-taught skills.**

💻 **Examples of Tech Careers:**

- ✔ **IT Support Specialist** ($40K–$75K per year)

- ✔ **Web Developer** ($50K–$100K per year)

- ✔ **Cybersecurity Analyst** ($60K–$120K per year)

- ✔ **Digital Marketer** ($50K–$100K per year)

- ✔ **Data Analyst** ($55K–$110K per year)

💰 **Why Choose This Path?**

- ☑ **Many jobs focus on skills, not degrees** – Companies hire based on what you can do.

- ☑ **Certifications are faster & cheaper than college** – Many take **a few months** instead of years.

- ☑ **Work-from-home options** – Many tech jobs allow remote work.

- ☑ **High earning potential** – Top tech fields offer six-figure salaries.

🚀 **How to Get Started:**

- ✔ Take **free or low-cost online courses** (Udemy, Coursera, Google IT Certs).

- ✔ Attend a **coding bootcamp** (3–9 months) for intensive training.

- ✔ Get an **entry-level IT job** and work your way up.

Public Service & First Responder Careers

Public service jobs offer **steady pay, great benefits, and strong pensions.** Many don't require college—just **academy training or certifications.**

🚓 **Examples of Public Service Jobs:**

✔ **Firefighter** ($45K–$100K per year)

✔ **Police Officer** ($50K–$95K per year)

✔ **EMT/Paramedic** ($40K–$75K per year)

✔ **Correctional Officer** ($40K–$80K per year)

✔ **Postal Service Worker** ($45K–$75K per year)

⚠ **Important Note:** Some government jobs **may** require some college credits, while others do not. **It depends on the jurisdiction.** For example:

✔ Some **police departments** require **an associate degree or a certain number of college credits** (but not a full degree).

✔ Some **fire departments and correctional agencies** may prefer candidates with **some college coursework** but don't require a full degree.

✔ **Federal jobs** often require a degree **or** relevant work experience (meaning you can qualify by working in the field first).

🚀 **How to Get Started:**

✔ Apply to a **fire or police academy** (usually a few months of training).

✔ Get certified as an **EMT** (3–6 months).

✔ Check for **government job openings** in your area.

Medical Careers Without a Degree

🏥 **Examples of Non-Degree Medical Jobs:**

 ✔ **Dental Hygienist** ($60K–$100K per year)

 ✔ **Pharmacy Technician** ($35K–$55K per year)

 ✔ **Ultrasound Technician** ($50K–$90K per year)

 ✔ **Medical Coding & Billing** ($40K–$75K per year)

 ✔ **Phlebotomist (Blood Draw Technician)** ($35K–$55K per year)

High-Value Sales: A High-Paying Job with No Degree Required

💲 **Examples of High-Paying Sales Careers:**

- ✔ **Real Estate Agent** ($50K–$250K+ per year)

- ✔ **B2B Sales (Business-to-Business)** ($60K–$200K per year)

- ✔ **Tech Sales (Software, SaaS, Cybersecurity, etc.)** ($80K–$300K per year)

- ✔ **Financial Services (Insurance, Investments, Mortgage Lending)** ($50K–$200K per year)

- ✔ **Luxury Sales (Cars, Jewelry, High-End Products)** ($50K–$150K per year)

🚀 **How to Get Started:**

- ✔ Consider **real estate or insurance sales**, which often require only a **state license** (no degree).

- ✔ Apply for **entry-level sales jobs** in industries like **tech, logistics, or finance.**

- ✔ Take **sales training courses** online or from industry professionals.

Final Thoughts on Career Options Without College

Skipping college **doesn't** mean settling for a low-paying job. **It means choosing a path that fits you—one where you can build skills, earn well, and succeed without a four-year degree.**

In the next section, we'll explore how you can **build your own career** through **entrepreneurship & freelancing**—because sometimes, the best job is the one you create for yourself.

📖 Section 2:
Entrepreneurship and Freelancing

Not everyone wants a traditional 9-to-5 job. Some people thrive when they **work for themselves, set their own schedule, and control their own income.**

The good news? You **don't need a degree** to be your own boss. Whether you're starting a **small business, freelancing, or launching an online brand,** there are countless ways to make money **without working for someone else.**

This section will cover:

- ☑ **Entrepreneurship** – Starting your own business

- ☑ **Freelancing** – Selling your skills without a traditional job

- ☑ **The Pros & Cons** of working for yourself

- ☑ **How to get started** with little to no money

Entrepreneurship: Creating Your Own Career

Entrepreneurship is about **building something of your own.** It could be a **physical business, an online store, a service, or a personal brand.** Many of the most successful entrepreneurs started with little more than an idea and the drive to make it work.

🚀 **Examples of Business Ideas You Can Start Without a Degree:**

- **Service-Based Businesses** – Landscaping, home cleaning, pressure washing, personal training, photography

- **Online Stores** – Dropshipping, print-on-demand, handmade crafts (Etsy), flipping products

- **Digital Businesses** – Social media management, consulting, YouTube, blogging, online courses

- **Local & Skilled Trades** – Car detailing, handyman services, mobile car repair, catering

💰 **Why Choose Entrepreneurship?**

☑ **Unlimited earning potential** – You control how much you make.

☑ **Be your own boss** – No one tells you what to do.

☑ **Flexibility** – Work when and where you want.

☑ **Job security** – No one can fire you if you own the business.

⚡ **Reality Check:**

- **It takes time to build success.** Most businesses don't take off overnight.

- **Income isn't guaranteed.** You have to put in the effort to bring in clients/customers.

- **You need to manage everything.** Marketing, finances, and customer service are all on you.

✏️ How to Get Started:

1. **Pick a business idea** – What can you offer that people will pay for?

2. **Start small** – Don't overcomplicate it. Just get your first customers.

3. **Market yourself** – Use social media, word of mouth, and local advertising.

4. **Learn as you go** – No one has all the answers at the start—just take action!

Freelancing: Getting Paid for Your Skills

Freelancing is a great way to **make money on your own terms** without starting a full business. Instead of working for one employer, you take on **clients and projects** as an independent worker.

🖥 Examples of Freelance Work:

- **Writing & Editing** – Articles, blogs, copywriting, resume writing
- **Graphic Design & Branding** – Logos, social media graphics, website design
- **Programming & Tech Services** – Web development, IT support, cybersecurity
- **Photography & Videography** – Events, portraits, social media content
- **Virtual Assistance** – Managing emails, scheduling, customer service
- **Tutoring & Online Teaching** – Test prep, language lessons, skill-based coaching

💰 Why Choose Freelancing?

- ✅ **You set your rates** – Charge what you're worth.
- ✅ **Choose your clients & projects** – Work on what interests you.
- ✅ **Work from anywhere** – Many freelance jobs are remote.
- ✅ **Low startup costs** – Most freelance work just requires a laptop and an internet connection.

⚡ **Reality Check:**

- **Freelance income isn't stable at first.** Some months will be busier than others.

- **You have to find your own clients.** No one hands you work—you have to market yourself.

- **No guaranteed benefits.** Unlike traditional jobs, there's no health insurance or retirement plan.

🚀 **How to Get Started:**

1. **Pick a skill** – What can you offer that businesses or individuals need?

2. **Set up a portfolio** – Show examples of your work (even if they're just practice projects).

3. **Create profiles on freelance websites** – Upwork, Fiverr, Free-lancer, etc.

4. **Reach out to potential clients** – Send emails, post on social media, and network.

The Pros & Cons of Being Your Own Boss

☑ **Pros:**

✓ You control your income – No waiting for promotions or pay raises.

✓ Flexible schedule – Work when and where you want.

✓ Creative freedom – Choose what kind of work you do.

✗ Cons:

✗ No guaranteed paycheck – You have to find clients/customers.

✗ More responsibility – Taxes, marketing, and customer service fall on you.

✗ It takes time – Many businesses take months (or even years) to grow.

Low-Cost Ways to Start a Business or Freelance Career

One of the biggest myths about starting your own business is that you need **a lot of money.** That's not true! Many successful businesses and freelance careers started with just **time, effort, and a little creativity.**

Ways to Start Without Much Money:

- **Service-Based Business:** Start with skills you already have (lawn care, tutoring, handyman work, babysitting).

- **Freelancing:** Offer services online (writing, web design, video editing, etc.).

- **Reselling:** Buy and flip items on eBay, Facebook Marketplace, or thrift stores.

- **Content Creation:** Start a YouTube channel, TikTok, or blog to build an audience and monetize later.

If you're **willing to put in the effort,** you can build something from **nothing**—without ever needing a college degree.

Final Thoughts on Entrepreneurship & Freelancing

If you don't want a traditional job, **you don't have to settle.**

If you want **flexibility, freedom, and unlimited earning potential,** working for yourself might be the best path.

It's not always easy, and it takes time, but with the right mindset and effort, you can **create your own career instead of waiting for someone to hire you.**

In the next section, we'll explore **alternative ways to learn and grow your skills without college**—because even if you don't go to school, **education never stops.**

📖 Section 3:
Alternative Learning Paths

Just because you're not going to college **doesn't mean you stop learning.** In fact, **learning is essential** if you want to grow in your career, start a business, or move into higher-paying roles.

The difference? **You don't have to spend four years and thousands of dollars to do it.**

There are **plenty of ways to gain valuable skills and certifications** without taking on college debt. In this section, we'll explore:

- **Apprenticeships & Trade Schools** – Hands-on learning with real-world experience
- **Employer-Paid Training Programs** – Companies that will pay you to learn
- **Industry Certifications** – Credentials that boost your job opportunities
- **Self-Directed Learning** – Free and low-cost ways to gain high-value skills

Apprenticeships & Trade Schools: Learn by Doing

Apprenticeships and trade schools offer **structured, hands-on training** that leads directly to jobs. Instead of sitting in a lecture hall, you **learn by working in the field—and** often **get paid while doing it.**

🛠 **Examples of Careers with Apprenticeships or Trade Schools:**

- **Electrician** (Apprenticeship required)
- **Plumber** (Apprenticeship required)
- **HVAC Technician** (Trade school or apprenticeship)
- **Carpenter** (Trade school or apprenticeship)
- **Welding** (Trade school certification)
- **Automotive Technician** (Trade school or on-the-job training)

💰 **Why Choose This Path?**

- ✅ **Fast track to a career** – Most programs last 6 months to 2 years.
- ✅ **Earn while you learn** – Many apprenticeships **pay you** while you train.
- ✅ **High job demand** – Skilled trades are always needed.
- ✅ **No massive student debt** – Apprenticeships are free or low-cost, and trade school is much cheaper than college.

🚀 **How to Get Started:**

- Search for **registered apprenticeships** on sites like **apprentice-ship.gov** (U.S.) or check local trade unions.

- Look for **local trade schools** that offer certifications in high-demand fields.

- Contact companies in the field and ask if they offer **on-the-job training programs.**

Employer-Paid Training Programs

Some companies **train you for free** as long as you agree to work for them after. This is a great option if you want to **learn a skill without paying for school.**

💼 **Examples of Jobs with Paid Training:**

- ✔ Commercial Trucking (CDL) – Some trucking companies cover your CDL training.

- ✔ IT & Tech Companies – Many large tech firms offer training for cybersecurity, networking, and IT support.

- ✔ Healthcare – Some hospitals train medical assistants, phlebotomists, or patient care techs.

- ✔ Manufacturing & Skilled Labor – Some companies train machinists, welders, or factory workers from scratch.

🚀 **How to Get Started:**

- ✔ Look up **"paid training jobs"** on job boards like **Indeed** or **LinkedIn.**

- ✔ Check **company websites** for workforce development programs.

- ✔ Call local **hospitals, manufacturing plants, or transportation companies** and ask about training opportunities.

Industry Certifications: A Fast, Affordable Way to Prove Your Skills

Industry certifications can **replace a degree in many fields.** These credentials show employers that you **know your stuff**—without spending four years in school.

Examples of In-Demand Certifications:

- **IT & Cybersecurity:** Google IT Support, CompTIA A+, Cisco CCNA, AWS Cloud

- **Project Management & Business:** PMP, Scrum Master, Six Sigma

- **Digital Marketing & E-Commerce:** Google Analytics, HubSpot, Facebook Blueprint

- **Medical & Healthcare:** Certified Medical Assistant, Phlebotomy Technician

- **Skilled Trades:** OSHA Safety, HVAC, Electrical Journeyman

Why Choose This Path?

Faster & cheaper than a degree – Most certifications take **weeks or months, not years.**

Boosts job opportunities – Many employers prefer certified candidates.

Helps you switch careers – Great if you want to move into a new industry.

How to Get Started:

- Search for **certifications in your industry** (many are offered online).

- Look at company job postings to see **which certifications they prefer.**

- Enroll in online courses on sites like **Coursera, Udemy, LinkedIn Learning.**

Self-Directed Learning: Teach Yourself High-Paying Skills

Some of the most successful people **never set foot in a classroom** after high school. Instead, they **taught themselves skills and built careers from scratch.**

📖 **Ways to Learn on Your Own:**

- **Online Courses & Bootcamps** – Udemy, Coursera, Skillshare, YouTube tutorials

- **Books & Audiobooks** – Read about business, sales, marketing, tech, or entrepreneurship

- **Internships & Volunteering** – Gain real-world experience for free

- **Building Your Own Projects** – If you want to be a **writer, designer, coder, or content creator**, start practicing and **create your own portfolio**

💲 **Why Choose This Path?**

☑ **No cost (or very low cost)** – Many resources are free or cheap.

☑ **Learn at your own pace** – No schedules, no deadlines.

☑ **Perfect for tech, creative, and business fields** – Many careers (like web development, graphic design, and social media marketing) don't require formal education—just skills.

🚀 **How to Get Started:**

- ✔ Pick **one skill** you want to learn.

- ✔ Find **free or cheap online courses.**

- ✔ Set a **weekly goal** for practice.

- ✔ Apply what you learn by **creating something real.**

177

Final Thoughts on Alternative Learning Paths

Skipping college **doesn't mean you stop learning.** It just means you're learning **in a smarter, faster, and more affordable way.**

Whether it's through **apprenticeships, certifications, online courses, or employer training,** you have **plenty of options** to build a great career without drowning in student debt.

In the next section, we'll cover **how to actually get hired without a degree**—because knowing the skills is one thing, but **proving your value to employers is what lands you the job.**

📖 Section 4:
Getting Hired Without a Degree

You have the skills. You've learned the trade, earned the certifications, or built a solid freelancing portfolio. Now, you just need one thing: **a job.**

The good news? **A degree is just one way to prove you're qualified—** but it's not the only way. Many employers care **more about what you can do** than a piece of paper saying you went to school.

This section will cover:

✓ **How to stand out on a résumé without a degree**

✓ **How to use networking to get hired faster**

✓ **How to ace interviews and prove your value**

✓ **How to negotiate pay and benefits**

How to Stand Out on a Résumé Without a Degree

Most people think their résumé has to start with 'Education.' **Not you.**

When you don't have a degree, **you highlight skills, experience, and results first.**

How to Format Your Résumé:

✓ **Skip the "Education" section** (or move it to the bottom).

✓ **Start with a strong 'Skills' section** – Highlight what you can actually do.

✓ **Use a 'Projects' or 'Certifications' section** – Show proof of your work.

✓ **List experience creatively** – If you don't have formal work experience, include freelance work, apprenticeships, internships, or personal projects.

How to Use Networking to Get Hired Faster

Most jobs **aren't even listed online—**they're filled through **word of mouth.** That's why networking is **so important.**

How to Network Like a Pro:

✓ **Talk to people in your industry.** Join **Facebook Groups, LinkedIn groups, or Reddit forums** in your field.

✓ **Attend local events & meetups.** Look for **career nights, job fairs, or industry networking events.**

✓ **Reach out directly.** Message hiring managers or business owners and ask for advice instead of just asking for a job.

🔩 How to Ace an Interview (Without a Degree)

Once you land an interview, **your job is to prove you can do the work.**

🏆 Interview Tips for Non-Degree Candidates:

✓ **Be confident** – Show employers that you are skilled and capable.

✓ **Show proof of your abilities** – Bring a portfolio, project samples, or certification documents.

✓ **Turn experience into results** – Instead of saying, "I worked on social media," say, "I helped a local brand grow from 500 to 5,000 followers in 3 months."

💰 How to Negotiate Pay & Benefits (Even Without a Degree)

Many employers **offer lower pay** to non-degree candidates—**unless you negotiate.**

How to Get Paid What You're Worth:

✓ **Do your research** – Look up average salaries on sites like **Glassdoor and Payscale.**

✓ **Talk about your results** – Employers pay for **value, not degrees.**

✓ **Be willing to ask** – Most employers **expect candidates to negotiate.**

Final Thoughts on Getting Hired Without a Degree

A degree is just one way to get a job—it's not the only way.

✓ If you have **skills, proof of work, and confidence,** you can land a great job.

✓ **Networking and hands-on experience matter more than a diploma.**

✓ **The best way to prove yourself is to show what you can do.**

In the next section, we'll explore **how to choose a career that's built to last—so you don't waste time in a job that disappears in 5 years.**

📖 Section 5: Future-Proof Careers and Industry Trends

The job market is always changing. New industries emerge, technology advances, and some jobs **disappear completely.**

If you're skipping college, you want to make sure you're not stepping into a **dead-end job.** You need a **future-proof career**—one that will stay in demand and **continue to grow** in the coming years.

This section will cover:

- ☑ **What makes a career future-proof?**
- ☑ **Industries that are growing fast**
- ☑ **Jobs that won't be replaced by AI or automation**
- ☑ **How to choose a career that lasts**

What Makes a Career Future-Proof?

A **future-proof job** is one that is:

✓ **In high demand** – Companies are actively hiring and struggling to find workers.

✓ **Not easily replaced by AI or robots** – Jobs that require human creativity, adaptability, or hands-on work are safer.

✓ **Flexible & evolving** – Jobs that allow you to learn new skills and shift as industries change.

🖋 **Examples of Careers at Risk of Automation:**

- ✗ Data entry clerks (AI can do it faster)
- ✗ Retail cashiers (Self-checkouts are replacing them)
- ✗ Some customer service roles (AI chatbots are taking over)
- ✗ Basic administrative assistants (Automated scheduling & AI tools are improving)

Industries That Are Growing Fast

These fields are **expanding rapidly** and offer **strong job security** for years to come.

1 Skilled Trades & Infrastructure Jobs

Why It's Future-Proof: Skilled labor is always needed, and most of these jobs **can't be automated.**

High-Demand Trades:

- **Electricians** ($50K–$90K per year)

- **Plumbers** ($50K–$100K per year)

- **Welders** ($40K–$85K per year)

- **HVAC Technicians** ($45K–$80K per year)

- **Heavy Equipment Operators** ($50K–$95K per year)

Why Choose This Path?

- These jobs are essential—**people always need heating, plumbing, and electricity.**

- They **can't be outsourced**—someone has to do the work locally.

- Demand is growing as **older tradespeople retire.**

2 Tech & Cybersecurity

Why It's Future-Proof: Tech is evolving **faster than ever,** and companies need skilled workers to **protect their data and systems.**

In-Demand Tech Jobs (No Degree Required):

- **IT Support Specialist** ($40K–$75K per year)

- **Cybersecurity Analyst** ($60K–$120K per year)

- **Cloud Computing Specialist** ($70K–$150K per year)

- **Data Analyst** ($55K–$110K per year)

- **Software Tester** ($50K–$100K per year)

Why Choose This Path?

- Many tech jobs **focus on skills, not degrees.**

- **Certifications** can replace a degree and get you hired faster.

- Cybersecurity & cloud computing jobs are growing **at twice the national average.**

3 Healthcare & Medical Support Jobs

Why It's Future-Proof: People will **always** need medical care. As the population ages, demand for healthcare workers is skyrocketing.

In-Demand Medical Jobs Without a Degree:

- **Dental Hygienist** ($60K–$100K per year)

- **Medical Assistant** ($40K–$65K per year)

- **Ultrasound Technician** ($50K–$90K per year)

- **Pharmacy Technician** ($35K–$55K per year)

- **Phlebotomist (Blood Draw Technician)** ($35K–$55K per year)

Why Choose This Path?

- Many healthcare jobs require **only certifications or a 1-2 year training program.**

- **Medical careers offer stability,** with thousands of job openings every year.

- Demand is **growing fast** as people live longer and need more healthcare services.

Green Energy & Environmental Careers

Why It's Future-Proof: As the world shifts to **renewable energy**, careers in solar, wind, and energy efficiency are booming.

High-Demand Green Jobs:

- **Solar Panel Installer** ($45K–$80K per year)

- **Wind Turbine Technician** ($50K–$100K per year)

- **Environmental Technician** ($40K–$80K per year)

- **Energy Efficiency Auditor** ($50K–$90K per year)

Why Choose This Path?

- The **renewable energy industry is growing rapidly.**

- Governments and companies are investing **billions** in green energy.

- Many positions require **only short-term training or apprenticeships.**

5 High-Value Sales & Business Development

💰 **Why It's Future-Proof:** As long as companies **need to make money,** they'll need salespeople to **bring in revenue.**

💰 **High-Paying Sales Careers (No Degree Required):**

- **Real Estate Agent** ($50K–$250K+ per year)

- **B2B Sales (Business-to-Business)** ($60K–$200K per year)

- **Tech Sales (Software, SaaS, Cybersecurity, etc.)** ($80K–$300K per year)

- **Financial Services (Insurance, Investments, Mortgage Lending)** ($50K–$200K per year)

- **Luxury Sales (Cars, Jewelry, High-End Products)** ($50K–$150K per year)

🚀 **Why Choose This Path?**

✅ Sales careers have **unlimited earning potential** with commission-based pay.

✅ **No degree required**—companies care about **results, not diplomas.**

✅ It teaches **transferable skills** (communication, persuasion, negotiation).

How to Choose a Career That Lasts

If you want job security **without a degree,** follow these **four steps:**

Step 1: Pick an industry that's growing.

> 🔍 Look for **job growth projections** on sites like the **Bureau of Labor Statistics (BLS).**

Step 2: Choose a job that can't be automated.

> 🤖 Avoid jobs that could be replaced by AI or machines.

Step 3: Find a skill that's in demand.

> 📈 If companies **struggle to hire** for a role, it means there's **high demand** and **great pay.**

Step 4: Keep learning & adapting.

> 🎓 Take **online courses, certifications, or apprenticeships** to **stay ahead of changes** in your industry.

Final Thoughts on Future-Proof Careers

Choosing a **future-proof career** means picking a job that will **still exist, grow, and pay well in the years ahead.**

> 💡 The best jobs without a degree **focus on skills, experience, and adaptability.**

In the next section, we'll talk about **money—how skipping college can set you up for financial success early on.**

📖 Section 6:
The Financial Advantages
of Skipping or Delaying College

One of the biggest benefits of skipping or delaying college is **financial freedom.**

While many people think of a college degree as a "safe investment," the reality is that **student debt, lost earning years, and high tuition costs** can put people at a financial disadvantage for decades.

This section will cover:

- ☑ **The cost of college vs. earning earlier**
- ☑ **How skipping student loans gives you a financial head start**
- ☑ **The power of investing early**
- ☑ **How delaying college can be a smarter choice**

The True Cost of College vs. Starting Work Earlier

Many students go to college because they're told it's the **"smart financial choice."** But let's break down the **real numbers.**

💲 Average Cost of College (4-Year Degree)

- **Public University (In-State):** $25,000–$35,000 per year ($100K–$140K total)
- **Private University:** $40,000–$60,000 per year ($160K–$240K total)
- **Lost Earnings While in School:** ~$30,000 per year (if you're not working full-time)
- **Student Loan Interest:** Adds $10K–$50K+ in extra costs over time

CAN'T I JUST SKIP COLLEGE?

📝 **Total Estimated Cost of a College Degree: $150,000–$300,000+**

📖 **Now, Compare That to Starting a Job or Trade at 18:**

- **Earn $40K–$60K per year right away**

- **Gain 4 years of real work experience**

- **Invest and save money instead of taking on debt**

🚀 **The Bottom Line:**

A 22-year-old with a college degree often has **$50K+ in student debt** and **no work experience.**

A 22-year-old who started working at 18 could have **$100K+ in earnings, work experience, and no debt.**

Which sounds like a better financial head start?

The Power of Avoiding Student Loan Debt

🎓 **How Much Do Student Loans Actually Cost You?**

Let's say you take out **$50,000 in student loans** at a **6% interest rate.**

- **Monthly Payment:** ~$550 per month
- **Time to Pay Off: 10–20 years**
- **Total Interest Paid: $10K–$30K+**

🏦 That's **hundreds of dollars a month** that could be going toward **a house, a car, or investments instead of loan payments.**

💲 **What Could You Do Without Student Loan Debt?**

☑ **Save for a house sooner**

☑ **Invest in retirement early**

☑ **Start your own business**

☑ **Have more financial freedom in your 20s and 30s**

The Power of Investing Early

📈 How Much Can Early Investing Grow?

Let's compare **someone who skips college and starts investing at 18** vs. **someone who goes to college and starts investing at 22.**

Person A (No College, Starts Investing at 18)

- Invests just **$300 per month**
- **7% average annual return**
- **At age 40: $350,000+**

Person B (Goes to College, Starts Investing at 22)

- Invests the same **$300 per month**
- **Same 7% return**
- **At age 40: $250,000+**

🚀 Why This Matters:

The person who **started investing at 18** has **$100,000 more** just because they started **four years earlier.**

This is the **power of compound interest**—your money makes money **faster when you start sooner.**

Delaying College: A Smarter Alternative

 Not sure if college is the right choice? You can always go later.

One of the biggest **misconceptions** is that you have to **go to college right after high school—or not at all.** That's **not true.**

 Reasons to Delay College:

✓ Try out different jobs before committing to a degree.

✓ Save money and pay for college **without student loans.**

✓ Build work experience that makes you more valuable to employers.

✓ Avoid wasting time (and money) on a degree you're not sure about.

 How to Make College More Affordable Later:

- Work for a company that **offers tuition reimbursement.**

- Attend community college first, then transfer.

- Pay cash for classes while working, instead of taking out loans.

🚀 **The Bottom Line:**

Not choosing college **right now** doesn't mean you're saying no forever. It just means you're choosing a **smarter, more affordable path.**

Final Thoughts on the Financial Benefits of Skipping or Delaying College

💡 **Skipping college (or delaying it) gives you:**

✓ **A massive financial head start** (no debt + early income)

✓ **More career flexibility** (you're not tied to one degree)

✓ **The ability to invest early and build wealth faster**

In the next section, we'll talk about **how to keep growing your career long-term—so you're not just getting a job, but building a future.**

📖 Section 7:
Career Growth and Long-Term Success Without a Degree

Getting your first job is just the beginning. The real key to **long-term success** is knowing **how to grow, adapt, and move up**—even without a degree.

This section will cover:

☑ **How to build a career roadmap** (set goals and level up)

☑ **The best ways to gain promotions and raises**

☑ **Certifications and training for career advancement**

☑ **How to pivot into higher-paying jobs over time**

Building Your Career Roadmap

A lot of people just **take a job and hope for the best.** But the people who grow into **high-paying, fulfilling careers** usually **plan ahead.**

🔍 How to Create a Career Roadmap:

1. **Pick a General Direction** – What industry do you want to be in? (Tech, skilled trades, sales, healthcare, etc.)

2. **Set a 1-Year Goal** – What's the next level? (Getting a promotion, learning a new skill, increasing income)

3. **Set a 5-Year Goal** – Where do you want to be? (Manager, business owner, top-level expert in your field)

4. **Identify Skills You Need** – What training or experience will help you move up?

Example Career Roadmap:

- **Start:** Entry-level IT Support job ($40K)

- **Year 1 Goal:** Earn Google IT Certification

- **Year 2 Goal:** Get promoted to Network Administrator ($60K)

- **Year 5 Goal:** Move into Cybersecurity ($90K+)

Why This Works:

- ✓ Instead of drifting from job to job, you're **working toward something bigger.**

- ✓ You know **what skills to focus on** to move up faster.

- ✓ Employers see you as **driven and goal-oriented**, which makes them invest in you.

How to Get Promotions & Pay Raises Without a Degree

🪶 **Want to move up faster? Here's how:**

☑️ **1. Be the person who solves problems.**

- The best way to get promoted? **Make your boss's job easier.**
- Take initiative, suggest improvements, and go the extra mile.

☑️ **2. Learn skills that make you more valuable.**

- If you're in **tech**, get a new certification.
- If you're in **trades**, master a specialty (like solar for electricians).
- If you're in **sales**, take a negotiation or leadership course.

☑️ **3. Ask for more responsibility (then prove yourself).**

- Volunteer to lead projects.
- Help train new employees.
- Show that you're **already doing the next job before you get the title.**

☑️ **4. Document your wins.**

- Keep track of how you've **helped the company.**
- Did you **save them money? Increase sales? Improve efficiency?**
- When it's time for a raise, **you have proof of your value.**

☑ 5. Negotiate your salary.

- Research industry pay rates.

- Show why you deserve a raise based on **results, not just time served.**

- If they can't give you a raise, **ask for new responsibilities or career growth opportunities.**

Certifications & Training for Career Advancement

Even if you don't have a degree, **certifications, online courses, and specialized training** can help you move up fast.

📃 Examples of Certifications for Career Growth:

🖥 Tech & IT:

- CompTIA Security+ (Cybersecurity)

- AWS Cloud Practitioner (Cloud Computing)

- Google Data Analytics

🛠 Skilled Trades:

- Master Electrician License
- HVAC Specialties (Geothermal, Refrigeration, etc.)
- OSHA Safety Certifications

📈 Business & Sales:

- HubSpot Sales Certification
- Dale Carnegie Sales Training
- Google Ads & Facebook Ads Certifications

🏥 Healthcare:

- Advanced EMT Training
- Pharmacy Technician Certification
- Medical Coding & Billing

🚀 How to Find the Best Certifications for Your Career:

- Check job listings to see **what certifications employers prefer.**
- Ask people in your field **which ones helped them get promoted.**
- Look for online programs that offer **flexible, affordable training.**

How to Pivot Into Higher-Paying Jobs Over Time

Your first job **doesn't have to be your forever job.** Many people **start in one field** and **use their skills to move into a higher-paying career.**

🚀 **How to Pivot to a Better Job:**

✅ **1. Identify Transferable Skills.**

- If you're in **customer service**, you already have **sales & communication skills.**

- If you're in **retail**, you have **inventory, management, and business skills.**

- If you're in **a trade**, you might be able to **start your own business.**

✅ **2. Gain Experience While Working.**

- Want to switch into **tech?** Get an entry-level IT certification while still working your current job.

- Want to move into **management?** Ask for leadership responsibilities where you are now.

- Want to start your own business? **Build it as a side hustle first.**

✅ **3. Network with People in Your Target Industry.**

- Connect with people on **LinkedIn, at industry events, or through online communities.**

- Learn from those who have **already made the switch.**

Example Career Pivots:

- **Retail Sales → Tech Sales → Software Sales ($150K+)**

- **Warehouse Worker → Logistics Coordinator → Supply Chain Manager ($100K+)**

- **Plumber → Plumbing Business Owner ($200K+)**

- **Freelance Graphic Designer → Marketing Director ($120K+)**

A Note About Career Ceilings Without a Degree

As you move up in your career, you might find that some industries or companies **require a degree for higher-level management positions.** This isn't always the case, but it's something to be **aware of as you plan your long-term goals.**

- ✓ Many companies **care more about experience than degrees**, but in some fields, having a diploma **may be required for leadership roles.**

- ✓ If you ever hit a ceiling, **there are workarounds**—such as getting **industry certifications, attending leadership training, or even pursuing a degree later on** (many companies offer tuition reimbursement).

- ✓ The key is to **know your industry and plan ahead** so you're never caught off guard.

🚀 **Bottom Line:**

Not having a degree **won't stop you from building a successful career**, but knowing where limitations **might** appear helps you **prepare in advance** and stay in control of your growth.

Final Thoughts on Career Growth Without a Degree

💡 **A degree isn't what gets you promoted—your skills, work ethic, and mindset do.**

✓ **Plan your career growth** like a roadmap, not just a series of random jobs.

✓ **Continuously build new skills** through certifications and hands-on learning.

✓ **Look for ways to add value** and make yourself indispensable to your company.

✓ **Be ready to pivot** into higher-paying roles as new opportunities arise.

📖 Final Thoughts and Action Steps

By now, you've seen that **a successful career without college is 100% possible**—but it doesn't just happen on its own.

Skipping college **doesn't mean less work.** It means **a different kind of work.**

Instead of spending four years in a classroom, you'll be:

- Learning through hands-on experience
- Earning certifications or industry-specific training
- Building a portfolio or proving your skills in real-world settings
- Networking and seeking out opportunities to advance

The path to success **without college** is about **taking control of your own career, continuously improving, and staying adaptable.** If you do that, you can **achieve just as much—if not more—than someone with a degree.**

What to Do Next: Your Action Plan

🚀 **Step 1: Choose Your Career Path**

- Do you want to work in **skilled trades, tech, healthcare, sales, or entrepreneurship?**

- Research what industries **interest you the most.**

🚀 **Step 2: Learn the Skills You Need**

- Look into **apprenticeships, certifications, or self-paced learning.**

- Find free or low-cost training options (**YouTube, Udemy, Coursera, Google, trade schools**).

🚀 **Step 3: Get Experience & Start Earning**

- Apply for **entry-level jobs or internships** in your chosen field.

- Offer **freelance or part-time services** to build your resume and skills.

- Join **networking groups, LinkedIn, and industry events** to connect with professionals.

Step 4: Keep Learning & Growing

- Take **higher-level certifications or training** as you advance.

- Look for **mentorship opportunities** from experienced professionals.

- Set **career goals** and keep pushing toward the next level.

A Final Word: Your Future Is in Your Hands

Skipping college **doesn't close doors—it opens different ones.**

But to succeed, **you have to be willing to put in the work.**

> **It's not about taking an "easier" route—it's about taking the route that fits YOU best.**

✓ If you stay **focused, proactive, and always learning**, you can build a **stable, high-paying, and fulfilling career**—without ever setting foot in a college classroom.

The opportunities are out there. **Go get them.**

-PART THREE-

CAN'T I JUST

HELP MY KID PICK A PATH?

*A Career + College Survival Guide for
Parents Who Want to Get It Right*

Jennifer Larsen

Originality Statement

This book is an original work written by the author and reflects their unique ideas, voice, and instructional approach. While it may reference common educational and career-planning concepts, all content, including structure, language, exercises, and framework, is the author's own creation. Any similarities to other published works are purely coincidental.

Printed in the United States of America

First Edition

Cover design by Rachel Bostwick

Interior design and layout by Rachel Bostwick

For information or bulk orders, visit cantijust.com

Contents

📖 Introduction:
Success Without College

◆ Helping Your Teen Navigate Their Future — Without the Pressure

If you're reading this, you're probably **trying to help your teenager figure out what comes next.**

✓ Maybe they have **no idea what they want to do.**

✓ Maybe they have **too many ideas.**

✓ Or maybe they're convinced they'll just **"figure it out later."**

Meanwhile, you're over here thinking,

?   *How do I help without pushing too hard?*

?   *How do I guide them without overwhelming them?*

?   *What if they make the wrong choice and regret it later?*

You're **not alone.** And if it feels harder to guide a teen into a **solid career path** than it was when we were their age, that's because **it is.**

◆ Why Career Planning Feels Harder Today

When we were growing up, the **path was more straightforward** for most people. There were **fewer career options, clearer job expectations, and college was far more affordable.**

Today, the world is different:

- ✓ **There are more career choices than ever,** but that also makes deciding harder.

- ✓ **College is expensive,** and many degrees don't guarantee high-paying jobs.

- ✓ **Teens feel pressure to "figure it all out" quickly,** even though most careers evolve over time.

- ✓ **The job market is unpredictable,** with automation, AI, and new industries constantly changing what's in demand.

And let's be honest – **teens don't always take advice well,** especially when it comes from their parents.

But here's the good news: **You don't need to have all the answers.** What your teen really needs is **support, encouragement, and someone who helps them ask the right questions.**

That's where this book comes in.

◆ How This Guide Will Help You (Without Adding Stress)

Your teen's main book is **designed to help them explore their strengths, interests, and career options.** But they'll get **so much more out of it if you're involved.**

◆ **Example:** Imagine your teen is trying to decide on an after-school activity. You could tell them **what to do** – or you could ask them:

> ✓ *"Would you rather do something hands-on or creative?"*

> ✓ *"Do you like working in a team or independently?"*

> ✓ *"What's something you've always been curious about but never tried?"*

The same strategy works for **career conversations.** Instead of pressuring them to "decide," you can **help them explore in a way that feels natural and low-stakes.**

◆ **How to Support Without Overstepping**

You don't have to **sit down and do assignments together** (unless you want to), but **a little engagement on your part can go a long way.**

Here's how you can help:

√ **Ask, don't dictate.** Instead of telling them what they should do, **ask what excites them, what they're curious about, and what skills they think they have.**

√ **Encourage self-reflection.** Teens often **overlook their own strengths.** Help them recognize what they do well – even things they don't see as "skills."

√ **Be open to different paths.** College is **great,** but it's not the only route to success. **Careers come in many forms, and fulfillment matters just as much as financial security.**

√ **Use this book as a conversation starter.** Ask about their thoughts on each section. *What surprised them? What ideas are standing out?*

◆ **Example:** If your teen is **great at problem-solving**, they might not realize that skill can be applied to **engineering, business, cybersecurity, or even event planning.** Helping them connect the dots **expands their career possibilities.**

Most importantly, **remind them that they don't have to figure it all out at once.** The goal isn't to **lock in a lifetime decision at 17** – it's to build a mindset that helps them **adapt, explore, and make informed choices along the way.**

☑ **Key Takeaway:** Your teen doesn't need a **perfect plan.** They just need **curiosity, confidence, and the freedom to explore without fear.**

◆ **You're Already Doing Something Right**

By reading this, you've already shown that you **care deeply about your teen's future.** That alone makes a huge difference.

◆ **Reminder for Parents:**

✓ **You don't need to be a career expert** – you just need to be **a supportive guide.**

✓ **Your teen doesn't need all the answers today.** Career paths evolve over time.

✓ **Your role is to help them explore, not pressure them into a decision.**

▣ **Key Takeaway:** You're not here to make choices **for them** – you're here to help them **discover what works for them.**

◆ **What's Next?**

In the next sections, we'll talk about:

✓ **How to understand your teen's perspective** (so they feel heard, not pressured).

✓ **How to have career conversations that open doors instead of shutting them down.**

✓ **How to support their exploration without micromanaging.**

◆ **Up Next: Understanding Your Teen's Perspective.**

📖 Section 1: Understanding Your Teen's Perspective

Helping your teen figure out their future can feel like a **daunting task** – especially when they seem **uninterested, overwhelmed, or unsure of where to start.** The truth is, most teens **don't have a clear picture of their future yet**, and that's **completely normal.**

Your role as a parent **isn't to hand them a fully mapped-out plan**, but to help them **start asking the right questions, exploring possibilities, and building the confidence to make decisions at their own pace.**

◆ **Why Teens Struggle with Career Decisions**

If you've ever asked your teen, **"What do you want to do when you grow up?"** and been met with a **shrug**, you're not alone. Today's teens face a world that's **very different from the one we grew up in.**

Some of the biggest challenges they face include:

◆ **1. Too Many Choices, Not Enough Direction**

When we were growing up, career paths seemed **simpler and more structured.** You went to college, learned a trade, or got a job and worked your way up. Today's teens have **more career options than ever** – but instead of making things easier, this often leads to **decision paralysis.**

◆ **Example:** A teen who enjoys technology might feel overwhelmed by the choices:

✓ Should they go into **coding, game design, cybersecurity, or IT support?**

✓ Should they **attend college, enroll in a bootcamp, or get a certification instead?**

✓ Will they make **the wrong choice and regret it later?**

233

☑ **How Parents Can Help:** Instead of asking **"What do you want to do?"**, help them **narrow their options** by focusing on their interests, skills, and long-term goals.

✦ **Better Questions to Ask:**

> ✓ *"What kinds of problems do you like solving?"*
>
> ✓ *"Would you rather work with people, technology, or ideas?"*
>
> ✓ *"What's something you'd love to learn more about?"*

✦ **2. Pressure to "Get It Right" the First Time**

Many teens believe that **their first career choice is permanent** – that if they don't pick the "perfect" path now, they'll be stuck.

✓ They hear messages like **"Choose wisely or you'll be paying for it forever"** (especially with the high cost of college).

✓ They see adults who **regret their career choices** and fear making the same mistake.

✓ They worry that **switching careers later means failure.**

◆ **Example:** A teen who loves art but worries they won't make enough money might feel stuck between:

✓ **Pursuing a passion** (graphic design, animation, illustration)

✓ **Choosing a "safe" degree** (business, marketing, or computer science)

✓ **Feeling paralyzed** because they don't want to make the wrong choice

How Parents Can Help: Remind them that **careers are not set in stone.** Many people **change fields multiple times**, and most skills **transfer between industries.**

◆ **Better Ways to Phrase It:**

✗ *"You need to pick a stable career and stick with it."*

✓ **Instead, try:** "Your first job doesn't have to be your forever job. It's okay to try different things and adjust along the way."

◆ **3. Limited Real-World Experience**

Many teens have **only been exposed to a handful of careers** – usually those of their parents, teachers, or professionals they've seen on TV. **Without firsthand experience, it's hard to know what different jobs are really like.**

◆ **Example:**

• A teen who **likes science** may assume **"doctor" is their only option** – but they might love careers in **forensic science, biotech, or lab research.**

• A teen interested in **fashion** might not realize that the industry includes **marketing, product development, styling, and costume design.**

How Parents Can Help:

✓ **Encourage career exposure** through job shadowing, volunteer work, or internships.

✓ **Introduce them to professionals** in different fields for informational interviews.

✓ **Suggest online research** – many careers have free resources, webinars, or "day in the life" videos.

✦ **Better Ways to Phrase It:**

✗ *"You need to decide what you want to do right now."*

✓ **Instead, try:** "You don't have to commit today – let's explore a few careers and see what interests you."

✦ **4. Conflicting Messages About What They "Should" Do**

Parents, teachers, social media, and society send mixed signals:

✓ **Follow your passion!**

✓ **Be practical!**

✓ **College is essential!**

✓ **Trade schools are better!**

✓ **Work for yourself!**

✓ **Work for stability!**

No wonder teens feel stuck. They're bombarded with advice that often **contradicts itself.**

✦ **Example:** A teen might hear:

- **From school counselors:** "Go to college – it's the best path."

- **From social media influencers:** "Skip college, start a business instead."

- **From parents:** "Just pick something stable and don't waste time."

How Parents Can Help:

✓ Instead of telling them **what they should do**, ask **what makes sense for them.**

✓ Guide them to **weigh the pros and cons** of different career paths.

✓ Remind them that **success looks different for everyone.**

Better Ways to Phrase It:

✗ *"You have to go to college to be successful."*

✓ **Instead, try:** "College is one option, but there are many ways to build a great career. Let's look at what makes the most sense for you."

◆ **The Balance Between Financial Security and Fulfillment**

One of the biggest conflicts parents and teens face is the **classic debate:**

    ✓ **Should they do what they love?**

    ✓ **Or should they focus on what makes money?**

Parents **want their kids to be financially secure,** and **teens want careers that excite them.** But the truth is, **these don't have to be opposites.**

☑ **How to Find the Middle Ground:**

    ✓ **Help your teen find careers that combine what they enjoy and what's in demand.**

    ✓ **Encourage skill-building.** Many careers **pay well if you develop specialized skills.**

    ✓ **Remind them that careers evolve.** Their first job won't define their whole life.

◆ **Better Ways to Phrase It:**

✗ *"You'll never make money doing that."*

✓ **Instead, try:** "Let's look at different ways you can turn your interests into a career that supports you."

◆ **What's Next?**

Now that we've covered **why career planning can be overwhelming for teens,** the next step is learning how to **talk about it in a way that helps rather than pressures them.**

In **Section 2**, we'll discuss:

> ✓ **How to ask career questions without making them feel judged.**

> ✓ **How to keep career conversations open and productive.**

> ✓ **Common mistakes parents make — and what to say instead.**

◆ **Up Next: Conversations That Help (and Ones That Hurt).**

📖 Section 2: Conversations That Help (and Ones That Hurt)

Talking to your teen about their future can feel like **walking a tightrope.**

      ✓ Say **too much,** and they shut down.

      ✓ Say **too little,** and they might drift without direction.

The key is asking the **right questions, listening more than advising,** and creating a space where they feel comfortable **exploring ideas — without fear of judgment or pressure.**

This section will help you **have more productive conversations** while avoiding common pitfalls that can make teens feel **pressured, discouraged, or misunderstood.**

◆ **How to Ask Questions That Spark Interest**

One of the best ways to guide your teen is to **help them think,** rather than **telling them what to do.**

> ✓ **Shift from** *"What do you want to do?"*
>
> ✓ **To:** *"What do you enjoy doing?"*

Many teens struggle with **career labels** but can easily talk about their **interests and strengths.** Instead of asking them to name a job, ask about:

- ✓ **Activities they enjoy** (creating, fixing things, helping people, organizing, analyzing, etc.).

- ✓ **Subjects or hobbies that interest them** (science, technology, sports, media, business, design, etc.).

- ✓ **Situations where they naturally excel** (leading, problem-solving, staying focused, working with their hands, etc.).

✦ **Example Parent-Teen Conversations**

> ✗ **Parent:** "You need to start thinking about your future. What do you want to do?"
>
> ✗ **Teen:** *[Shrugs]* "I don't know."
>
> ✗ **Parent:** "Well, you have to choose something! You can't just wait forever."

⊖ *Why this doesn't work:* It puts **pressure on them** without giving them a starting point.

✓ Better Approach:

✓ **Parent:** "You don't have to know your exact career yet, but let's start with something easier – what kinds of things do you enjoy working on?"

✓ **Teen:** "I like figuring out how things work."

✓ **Parent:** "That's great! Some careers focus on problem-solving – engineering, coding, even forensic science. Want to explore a few of those?"

Why this works: Instead of demanding an answer, it **helps them reflect** and **explore possibilities.**

◆ **How to Point Out Strengths Without Sounding Like You're Pushing**

Sometimes, **teens don't see their own strengths** because they assume:

✓ *"It's easy for me, so it must not be a real skill."*

✓ *"I just like doing it – I never thought of it as a career."*

📌 **Example:** A teen who **loves organizing things** may not realize that could lead to careers in **event planning, logistics, or operations management.**

How to naturally introduce career possibilities without making it feel forced:

✓ **Parent:** "You're really great at organizing things. Have you ever thought about careers where that could be useful?"

✓ **Teen:** "Like what?"

✓ **Parent:** "Well, event planners, project managers, and even film producers need those skills. Want to check out how those jobs work?"

✅ *Why this works:* It introduces career ideas **without forcing them into a decision.**

◆ **Common Pitfalls That Shut Down Career Conversations**

Even well-intended advice can accidentally make your teen **shut down or feel pressured.** Here are some phrases to avoid – and **better alternatives.**

✕ **"You'll never make money doing that."**

✓ **Instead, try:** "That's an interesting field. Have you looked into the different career paths related to it?"

◆ **Why?** Even careers that seem impractical often have **profitable niches.** Instead of shutting them down, help them explore **options within their interests.**

◆ **Example:** If your teen loves **writing**, don't dismiss it as "impractical." Instead, explore **high-paying writing careers** like **technical writing, copywriting, UX writing, or publishing.**

✕ **"Just go to college and figure it out later."**

✓ **Instead, try:** "College is one option, but let's think about what you actually want to do first."

◆ **Why?** College is a **huge investment**, and going in without a plan can lead to **wasted time and money.** Encourage them to **explore careers before committing to a degree.**

◆ **Better Approach:**

   ✓ **Parent:** "If college is part of your plan, let's check which careers require a degree and which don't. That way, you can make a smart choice about your education."

✕ **"I know what's best for you."**

✓ **Instead, try:** "I want to help you find a path that makes sense for you. Let's figure it out together."

✦ **Why?** Even if you have valuable insights, teens need to feel like they have **control over their own future.**

✦ **Example:**

 ✓ Instead of saying, *"You should go into business because it's safe,"*

 ✓ Try, *"You seem interested in leadership and strategy – have you thought about business or marketing?"*

▨ *Why this works:* It presents career ideas **without making them feel forced into a path.**

◆ **How to Keep the Conversation Open and Supportive**

◆ **1. Listen More Than You Speak**

If your teen is willing to **talk about their future,** resist the urge to **jump in with advice too quickly.** Sometimes, they just need to **talk it out first.**

> ✓ Let them **express their thoughts** before offering input.

> ✓ Ask **follow-up questions** instead of giving immediate solutions.

◆ **2. Be Patient with Uncertainty**

It's okay if they **don't have a clear answer yet.** Encourage them to:

> ✓ Try **different experiences** (internships, courses, job shadowing).

> ✓ Explore **multiple career options** instead of locking into one path.

◆ **Example:**

✓ Instead of saying, *"You need to decide already,"*

✓ Try, *"It's okay if you're still figuring things out. Let's find ways for you to explore different careers before making a decision."*

3. Check In Periodically, Not Just Once

Career exploration **isn't a one-time conversation** – it's an **ongoing process.**

✓ Keep the dialogue open by **checking in casually** rather than having **one big pressure-filled talk.**

Example: Instead of, *"We need to have a serious talk about your future,"*

   ✓ Try bringing it up **naturally in everyday situations**, like:

   ✓ *"I saw an article about someone who turned their love of gaming into a career – want to check it out?"*

   ✓ *"I just met someone who works in cybersecurity – want to hear what they said about their job?"*

Why this works: **Low-pressure conversations** keep career discussions **open and ongoing.**

◆ **What's Next?**

Even with open, productive conversations, some teens **still feel anxious about making career choices.** The pressure to **"get it right"** can make them feel **paralyzed or uncertain.**

In the next section, we'll discuss:

> ✓ **Why career anxiety is so common for teens today.**

> ✓ **How to support a teen who's feeling overwhelmed.**

> ✓ **Ways to help them move forward, even if they're afraid of making the wrong choice.**

◆ **Up Next: Handling Teen Anxiety About Career Choices.**

📖 **Section 3:
Handling Teen
Anxiety About Career Choices**

❖ Why Career Anxiety is So Common for Teens

If your teen is feeling **overwhelmed, stuck, or even avoiding career conversations altogether**, you're not alone. Career anxiety is **more common than ever** because today's teens are facing:

✓ **More choices than ever before** – The sheer number of career paths can lead to **decision paralysis.**

✓ **Pressure to make the "right" choice immediately** – Teens feel like they have to **pick a lifelong career** at 17.

✓ **Fear of failure** – They're afraid of **choosing wrong** and ending up unhappy or unsuccessful.

✓ **Social comparison** – Social media makes it easy to compare their progress to peers who seem to have it all figured out.

✓ **Worries about money** – Rising college costs and student loan debt make career decisions feel **high-stakes.**

Many parents see this anxiety as a lack of motivation – but it's often the opposite. Some teens shut down because they **care so much about making the right choice that they're afraid to choose anything.**

📋 **Key Takeaway:** If your teen is struggling with career anxiety, they don't need **pressure to decide – they need reassurance that they can explore, test, and change paths as they grow.**

◆ **Signs Your Teen is Struggling with Career Anxiety**

Some teens **talk openly about their fears,** but others **keep them bottled up.** Watch for these common signs of career-related stress:

◆ **Signs of Career Anxiety:**

  ✖ **Avoids career discussions** – Changes the subject or shrugs off questions about the future.

  ✖ **Feels paralyzed by indecision** – Says, *"I don't know,"* but also avoids exploring options.

  ✖ **Expresses fear of failure** – Worries about *"picking the wrong career"* or *"ruining their life"* with one bad choice.

  ✖ **Compares themselves to others** – Feels behind because *"everyone else knows what they're doing."*

  ✖ **Obsesses over the "perfect" choice** – Won't commit to anything because they think there's *one right answer.*

◆ **Example:** A teen who **loves writing** might feel anxious because they've heard **"writers don't make money."** Instead of exploring related careers (journalism, marketing, UX writing), they **shut down** because they think their interests won't lead to success.

☑ **Key Takeaway:** Career anxiety **isn't about laziness – it's about fear of making the wrong choice.** Your teen may need **encouragement, perspective, and real-world exposure** to move past these fears.

- **How to Help an Anxious Teen Navigate Career Choices**

If your teen is feeling overwhelmed, here's how to **help them move forward without pressure:**

✓ **Normalize Uncertainty** – Let them know that **most adults don't have everything figured out either.**

✓ **Encourage Small Steps Instead of Big Decisions** – Career choices aren't **all or nothing.** They can **test different options through internships, part-time work, or courses.**

✓ **Expose Them to Career Possibilities** – Sometimes, anxiety comes from **not knowing what's out there.** Help them explore jobs through **shadowing, networking, or career fairs.**

✓ **Help Them Separate Interests from Careers** – If they love something but don't see a career path, help them **connect the dots** to industries that use those skills.

- **Example Conversations:**

Teen: "I have no idea what I want to do."

Parent: "That's totally okay. Most people don't figure it out right away. What's something you've been curious about?"

Teen: "I don't want to pick the wrong career."

Parent: "No career choice is permanent. Plenty of people switch paths over time. Let's look at careers where your skills can transfer."

Teen: "I don't know how to choose between all these options."

Parent: "Let's break it down. What's something you'd actually enjoy learning more about?"

* **Final Thought: Career Anxiety Fades with Action**

The best way to **ease career anxiety** is to **take small steps.** Your teen doesn't have to **choose today** – they just need to **start exploring.**

☑ **Encourage curiosity over commitment.**

☑ **Remind them that careers evolve over time.**

☑ **Help them focus on next steps, not final answers.**

* **What's Next?**

Now that we've covered **why career anxiety is common and how to help your teen move past fear,** the next step is ensuring they engage with their career guide in a way that feels **helpful, not overwhelming.**

◆ **Up Next: How to Help Your Teen Use the Main Book.**

📖 Section 4:
How to Help Your Teen
Use the Main Book

Even the **best career guidance book** won't be useful if it just **sits on a shelf.** But let's be honest – most teens **aren't going to eagerly dive into a self-reflection workbook on their own.**

That's where you come in.

Your role **isn't to make them do every exercise** or treat this like another school assignment. Instead, it's about **helping them engage with the book** in a way that feels **natural, useful, and even – dare we say – interesting.**

◆ How to Get Them Started (Without Forcing It)

If you push too hard, your teen might **resist engaging** with the book. Instead, try these strategies to make the process **feel natural.**

◆ 1. Give Them Space to Explore on Their Own First

Some teens will **resist anything that feels like a "parent-led" project.** Instead of presenting this as a **must-do task,** keep it casual.

◆ Example:

✓ Instead of, *"You need to read this book and do the exercises,"*

✓ Try, *"I found this book and thought it might help. No pressure, but if you check it out, I'd love to hear what you think."*

Why this works: This approach makes them **feel in control** rather than feeling like it's another assignment.

◆ 2. Make It a Conversation, Not an Assignment

Instead of **asking whether they've "done the exercises"**, use the book as a **jumping-off point for discussions.**

* **Example:**

  ✓ **Parent:** "I was flipping through the book and found the section on strengths really interesting. What did you think?"

  ✓ **Teen:** "I haven't looked at it yet."

  ✓ **Parent:** "No worries! One of the questions was about skills you don't even realize you have. I was thinking about mine – want to guess what they are?"

Why this works: It **keeps the conversation casual** while sparking curiosity.

* **3. Share Your Own Experiences**

Teens often resist career conversations because they feel like **they're the only ones struggling.** Sharing **your own career journey** can make them feel **less pressured** and more willing to explore.

* **Example Parent Dialogue:**

  ✓ **Parent:** "When I was your age, I had no idea what I wanted to do. I picked a major just because I thought it was practical, but later realized I actually loved something else."

  ✓ **Teen:** "Really? What did you switch to?"

  ✓ **Parent:** "Marketing! I started in finance, but I realized I loved the creative side of business more. I wish I had explored my options earlier."

Why this works: It shows that **career paths aren't set in stone** and that **exploration is normal.**

◆ **Ways to Keep Your Teen Engaged with the Book**

If your teen starts using the book but **loses interest**, here are **ways to keep them engaged.**

◈ 1. Tie the Book to Real-Life Experiences

Teens will be **more motivated** to explore careers when they see **real-world connections.**

◈ Example:

- ✓ If they're interested in **sports**, show them careers beyond being an athlete, like **sports management, physical therapy, or coaching.**
- ✓ If they enjoy **gaming**, introduce careers in **game design, coding, or streaming.**

How to connect the book to real life:

- ✓ If they read about a career that **sparks interest,** look up **day-in-the-life videos** on YouTube.
- ✓ If they complete a **strengths or interests exercise**, brainstorm **careers that align with their results.**

◈ 2. Turn It into a Fun Challenge

If your teen is **reluctant to do the exercises**, turn them into a **friendly game.**

◈ Example:

- ✓ **Parent:** "Let's both do the 'Hidden Skills' exercise and compare answers – want to see if we come up with the same ones for you?"

263

✓ **Teen:** "Okay, but only if I get to guess yours too."

☑ *Why this works:* It **removes the pressure** and makes it feel **interactive.**

✦ 3. Celebrate Small Wins, Not Just the Final Answer

Teens don't have to **figure out their entire future overnight.** Encourage **small steps** and celebrate their progress.

✦ Example:

✓ Instead of asking, *"Have you picked a career yet?"*

✓ Say, *"You've been exploring different fields – what's something new you've learned about yourself?"*

☑ *Why this works:* It shifts the focus from **pressure to progress.**

✦ What If They Seem Uninterested?

Not every teen will **immediately engage** with the book, and that's okay. Here's what **not to do** – and what to try instead.

✕ Don't: Nag or Force a Schedule

✓ **Instead, try:** Leaving the book accessible and casually checking in.

✦ **Example:** *"I know you're busy, but if you ever want to look at that career book, it's on the table."*

✕ Don't: Dismiss Their Resistance

✓ **Instead, try:** Asking why they're hesitant.

✦ **Example:**

  ✓ **Parent:** "I noticed you haven't looked at the book yet – does something about it feel unhelpful?"

  ✓ **Teen:** "I just don't know where to start."

  ✓ **Parent:** "That's totally fair. Want to go through one part together?"

✕ Don't: Make It a High-Stakes Discussion

✓ **Instead, try:** Keeping it **low-pressure and natural.**

✦ **Example:**

  ✓ Instead of, *"You need to decide your future,"*

  ✓ Try, *"No rush, but I'd love to hear what's interesting to you so far."*

Why this works: It keeps **career exploration light and approachable.**

◆ **Making This a Team Effort**

Some teens **may not dive into the book on their own** – but they might be **more interested** if they see you participating.

◆ **Ways to Make It a Shared Experience:**

✓ **Try an exercise yourself first.** Fill out one of the self-reflection questions and share your answers.

✓ **Discuss topics over a casual meal.** Ask open-ended questions about the book's concepts.

✓ **Use it to spark outside activities.** If your teen reads about a career they like, suggest a job shadowing opportunity or a related project.

◆ **Example Parent Dialogue:**

✓ **Parent:** "I just did the 'What Skills Do You Have?' exercise. Turns out, I'm good at explaining things – maybe I should have been a teacher!"

✓ **Teen:** "Really? I never thought about that for you."

✓ **Parent:** "Yeah! Want to take a look and see what skills you might not realize you have?"

Why this works: It makes the book **interactive and engaging**, rather than a solo task.

◆ **What's Next?**

The more your teen **engages with career exploration,** the better they'll understand **themselves and their options.**

But beyond the book, **there's another key factor in making great career choices — real-world exposure.**

◆ **Up Next: Exposing Your Teen to Real-World Career Options.**

📖 Section 5:
Exposing Your Teen to
Real-World Career Options

No matter how many career books, personality tests, or interest surveys your teen completes, **nothing replaces real-world experience.**

The best way to help them make **informed career choices** is to expose them to as many **different experiences as possible** – giving them a chance to see what they enjoy, what they're naturally good at, and what feels right for them.

Think of it like **introducing a child to different foods.** You don't expect them to love everything they try, but the more they're exposed to, the better they understand their preferences. **The same goes for careers** – the more they experience, the more confidently they can choose.

◆ **Why Career Exposure Matters**

Many teens **only have a vague idea** of what careers actually involve. They might say they want to be a **lawyer, doctor, or engineer** because those are familiar job titles – but do they really know **what a day in those jobs looks like?**

◆ **How Exposure Helps Your Teen:**

✓ **Seeing a career in action is different from reading about it.** A teen might think they want to work in a hospital, but after shadowing a nurse, they realize they **can't stand the sight of blood.** Or they might not consider engineering, but after visiting a robotics lab, they **discover a passion for design.**

✓ **It helps them discover what they love (and what they don't).** Exposure isn't just about finding the **right** career – it's also about eliminating options that **don't** fit. The earlier they figure that out, the fewer detours they'll take later.

✓ **It makes career decisions feel less abstract.** Many teens struggle to answer *"What do you want to do?"* because they don't have enough context to make an informed decision. Giving them **hands-on experiences** turns vague ideas into real possibilities.

◆ Ways to Give Your Teen Career Exposure

You don't have to **orchestrate grand experiences** – sometimes, the best insights come from small, everyday opportunities.

Here are **practical ways** to help your teen explore careers in a way that feels **natural and engaging.**

◆ 1. Encourage Job Shadowing

A few hours **watching someone work** can provide **valuable insight** into what a job is really like.

◆ Example:

- ✓ A teen interested in **medicine** might shadow a **doctor, nurse, or EMT.**
- ✓ A teen drawn to **law** could spend a day with a **paralegal or courtroom assistant.**
- ✓ A **tech-focused teen** might observe an **IT specialist or software developer.**

☑ How Parents Can Help:

- ✓ Ask **friends, family, or local businesses** if they'd allow your teen to shadow for a day.
- ✓ Check if **high schools or career centers** offer shadowing programs.
- ✓ Encourage your teen to **reach out on their own** – learning to network is a valuable skill!

◆ Example Parent-Teen Dialogue:

- ✓ **Parent:** "I know you've been interested in marketing. Would you want to shadow my coworker who does social media management?"

272

✓ **Teen:** "Maybe. What do they do?"

✓ **Parent:** "They handle brand accounts, run ad campaigns, and create content. It might be a good way to see if that side of business interests you."

Why this works: It introduces **career exposure naturally** and gives the teen **a choice.**

⟐ 2. Help Them Find Internships or Part-Time Jobs

Even if it's **not their dream job**, working in different environments **teaches valuable skills.**

⟐ Example:

✓ **Retail or food service jobs** teach **customer service, teamwork, and problem-solving.**

✓ **Office jobs** expose teens to **business operations, scheduling, and communication.**

✓ **Internships (paid or unpaid)** provide **real-world industry experience.**

How Parents Can Help:

✓ Check **local businesses, community programs, and school counselors** for opportunities.

✓ Help them **write a simple email** to ask about openings.

✓ Encourage them to **start small** – even short-term work experience is beneficial.

Example Parent-Teen Dialogue:

✓ **Teen:** "I don't want to work in fast food forever."

✓ **Parent:** "I get that. But having a job teaches responsibility. Plus, customer service skills are useful in almost every career."

✓ **Teen:** "Like how?"

✓ **Parent:** "Even if you become a doctor or business owner, you'll still need to communicate well with people. It's all connected."

Why this works: It **reframes work experience as valuable,** even if it's not the teen's dream job.

3. Visit Different Workplaces

If you have the chance, take your teen to **a variety of work environments** – places they might not otherwise see.

Examples of Workplaces to Visit:

✓ **A hospital or medical center** – Great for teens considering **healthcare careers.**

✓ **A news station or creative agency** – Helps teens see jobs in **media, marketing, and journalism.**

✓ **A construction site or manufacturing plant** – Ideal for those interested in **engineering, trades, or industrial work.**

274

✓ **A courtroom** – Gives insight into **legal and government careers.**

■ **How Parents Can Help:**

> ✓ If you have a **"Take Your Child to Work Day"**, use it as an opportunity!

> ✓ Call local businesses and ask if they **offer student tours.**

> ✓ Attend **career fairs or job expos** with them.

✦ **Example Parent-Teen Dialogue:**

✓ **Parent:** "There's a tech company nearby that's doing an open house next week. Want to check it out?"

✓ **Teen:** "What would I even do there?"

✓ **Parent:** "Meet some employees, see how they work, and maybe get ideas for future careers. No pressure, just an opportunity to explore."

■ *Why this works:* It keeps career exploration **low-pressure and interactive.**

✦ **4. Encourage Hands-On Hobbies**

Sometimes, hobbies reveal **hidden career paths.**

✦ **Examples of Hobbies That Connect to Careers:**

✓ **Video editing** → Digital marketing, film production, YouTube content creation

✓ **Coding games for fun** → Software development, cybersecurity, game design

✓ **Fixing cars** → Mechanical engineering, auto repair, racing industry

✓ **Organizing school events** → Event planning, project management, hospitality

How Parents Can Help:

✓ Support **projects, clubs, or competitions** related to their interests.

✓ Encourage **side gigs** – selling art, designing websites, tutoring, etc.

✓ Help them connect **passions to potential career fields.**

Example Parent-Teen Dialogue:

✓ **Parent:** "I noticed you've been editing videos for fun. Did you know video editing is a career?"

✓ **Teen:** "Really? I just do it for fun."

✓ **Parent:** "Lots of industries need video editors – marketing, social media, even film production. Want to check out what it takes to go pro?"

Why this works: It helps teens see **their natural interests as potential career paths.**

◆ **Final Thought: Exposure Makes Career Choices Easier**

The more **careers your teen experiences firsthand**, the easier it will be for them to **decide what feels right**.

◆ **How Parents Can Support Career Exploration:**

✓ Encourage **curiosity over commitment.**

✓ Provide **exposure without pressure.**

✓ Celebrate **every step forward — even small ones.**

◆ **What's Next?**

Exposure is one of the best tools for career discovery, but what comes next?

In the next section, we'll talk about how to help your teen **sort through their experiences and make choices** – without overwhelming them or rushing the process.

◆ **Up Next: College, Trade School, or Straight to Work?**

📖 Section 6:
College, Trade School, or Straight to Work?

For a long time, the path after high school seemed **simple**:

✓ Go to college.

✓ Get a degree.

✓ Get a job.

But today, it's **not so clear-cut.**

✓ **College is more expensive than ever.** Parents and teens are rightfully concerned about student debt and whether a degree will actually **pay off.**

✓ **Skilled trades and alternative paths are gaining recognition.** Many high-paying jobs **don't require a four-year degree.**

✓ **The job market is unpredictable.** Some degrees **lead directly to careers**, while others don't. Meanwhile, **new industries are emerging all the time.**

With all these factors, it's no wonder teens feel **overwhelmed** by the choice.

Your role as a parent **isn't to decide for them** but to help them **weigh their options in a way that fits their strengths, interests, and goals.**

 ◆ **Understanding the Options (Without Bias)**

Each path has **pros and cons**, and what works for one teen **may not work for another.**

Here's a **balanced breakdown** of each option:

 ◆ **1. College (2-Year or 4-Year Degree)**

 Best for:

  ✓ Careers that **require** specialized education (**medicine, law, engineering, teaching**).

  ✓ Those who enjoy **academic learning** and want the **structured college experience.**

  ✓ Fields where a degree is **required for career advancement.**

 Financial Considerations:

  ✓ Private colleges **can be expensive,** but some offer **more financial aid.**

  ✓ In-state public universities **tend to be more affordable** than out-of-state options.

  ✓ Community college **can be a smart first step** before transferring to a four-year school.

⚠ Potential Downsides:

✓ Not all degrees lead directly to **high-paying jobs.**

✓ Many students **graduate with debt** but without clear career direction.

✓ Some careers require **more than just a degree** – internships, networking, and hands-on experience are just as important.

✦ Example:

✓ A student who loves **science** and wants to be a **physical therapist** would likely need **a college degree + graduate school.**

✓ A student who enjoys **business** might not need a degree if they focus on **entrepreneurship or certifications.**

☑ Parent Discussion Idea:

✓ Instead of saying, *"You have to go to college,"*

✓ Try, *"Let's research which careers actually require a degree and which don't."*

✦ 2. Trade Schools & Apprenticeships

✕ Best for:

✓ Hands-on learners who prefer **practical, skills-based work.**

✓ High-demand fields like **electricians, mechanics, plumbing, HVAC, welding, IT technicians.**

✓ Students who want to **start earning quickly** without a four-year commitment.

⚱ Financial Considerations:

✓ Trade schools **cost significantly less** than college.

✓ Many apprenticeship programs **pay students while they learn.**

✓ Skilled trades often have **high job security and good salaries.**

⚠ Potential Downsides:

✓ Some trades require **physical labor or location-based work.**

✓ Fewer career shifts than a broad college degree might allow.

✦ Example:

✓ A teen who enjoys **fixing cars and working with their hands** might thrive as an **auto mechanic or machinist.**

✓ A student who loves **technology** but doesn't want a traditional college route could explore **cybersecurity or IT certifications.**

☑ Parent Discussion Idea:

✓ Instead of saying, *"College is the only way to make money,"*

✓ Try, *"Let's check out salary data for trade jobs vs. college degrees and compare earning potential."*

◆ 3. Straight to Work (Entry-Level Jobs & On-the-Job Training)

💼 Best for:

✓ Teens who want to **gain work experience immediately** and explore careers through employment.

✓ Industries that offer **growth opportunities without a degree** (sales, tech, marketing, real estate).

✓ Those who plan to **earn and save before deciding on college or training.**

💲 Financial Considerations:

✓ Immediate income with **no student debt.**

✓ Some companies offer **tuition reimbursement** for future education.

✓ Can allow time to **test different career paths before committing.**

⚠ Potential Downsides:

✓ Some entry-level jobs **don't pay well at first.**

✓ Career growth may be **slower without specialized training or education.**

◆ Example:

✓ A teen unsure about their future could **work in customer service or retail** while exploring interests.

✓ A student who's great at **persuasion and people skills** might go straight into **sales or real estate.**

🗒 Parent Discussion Idea:

✓ Instead of saying, *"You need to pick a career before graduating,"*

✓ Try, *"If you're unsure, let's explore jobs that help you gain skills while figuring things out."*

CAN'T I JUST HELP MY KID PICK A PATH?

How to Help Your Teen Choose (Without Pushing One Way)

It's easy to default to our own views on **education and career paths,** but the best approach is to **help your teen consider the facts.**

1. Ask About Their Long-Term Goals

✓ Instead of **pushing a decision**, guide them to think about the future.

Example Parent Dialogue:

✓ **Parent:** "What kind of work sounds fulfilling to you?"

✓ **Teen:** "I like working with technology."

✓ **Parent:** "Great! Let's look at tech careers that require a degree vs. those that don't."

2. Research Career Salaries and Job Demand Together

✓ Show them how to compare **career salaries, job openings, and education requirements.**

Example:

✓ A student considering **graphic design** can explore whether they need a **degree or if certifications + portfolio work are enough.**

3. Encourage Test Runs Before Committing

✓ **Before enrolling in a program**, see if they can **shadow a professional, do an internship, or take an introductory course.**

Example:

✓ If your teen wants to study **psychology**, they might first work as a **behavioral aide or volunteer in a counseling setting.**

4. Discuss Finances Openly

✓ Help them understand the **financial side of each path** – without fear or pressure.

Example Parent Dialogue:

✓ **Parent:** "Let's compare what college will cost and what kind of salary you can expect after graduation."

✓ **Teen:** "I didn't realize some degrees don't lead to high salaries."

✓ **Parent:** "Yeah, it's good to check that before taking on loans."

◆ **What's Next?**

Making an informed decision about **college, trade school, or going straight to work** isn't just about what sounds appealing – it's also about **understanding the financial realities of each path.**

In the next section, we'll explore:

✓ **The true cost of college and how to make it more affordable.**

✓ **Alternatives to traditional four-year programs that can still lead to great careers.**

✓ **Smart financial decisions teens (and parents) can make now to set them up for future success.**

◆ **Up Next: Understanding College Costs & Smart Financial Choices.**

📖 Section 7: Understanding College Costs & Smart Financial Choices

◆ The Reality: College is Expensive – But There Are Options

For many families, **college costs are one of the biggest concerns** when discussing career options.

✓ **Student loan debt is at an all-time high.**

✓ **Not every college degree leads to high-paying jobs.**

✓ **Many students don't realize all the ways to make college more affordable.**

Key Takeaway: Instead of assuming **college is all or nothing,** parents and teens should explore **all the financial options available** to make a **smart, cost-effective decision.**

◆ **How to Help Your Teen Make a Financially Smart College Choice**

✓ **Compare Costs Between Schools** – The price difference between **in-state vs. out-of-state, private vs. public, or community college vs. university** can be **huge.**

✓ **Look for Schools That Offer the Best Aid** – Some expensive private schools **offer more scholarships than public ones.**

✓ **Encourage Part-Time & Alternative Paths** – Some students **work while attending college part-time** to minimize debt.

✓ **Consider Community College First** – Two years of community college before transferring can **save thousands of dollars.**

◆ **Example Cost Breakdown:**

A student attending **community college for 2 years, then transferring** to a state university **could save $20,000–$40,000** compared to four years at a university.

◆ **Other Ways to Reduce Costs:**

✓ **Online Degree Programs** – Often more flexible & lower-cost.

✓ **Employer Tuition Assistance** – Some companies will pay for a degree if you work there.

✓ **Work-Study & Paid Internships** – Earn money while gaining experience.

◆ **Helping Your Teen Make a Smart Investment**

College is **only worth the cost if it leads to real opportunities.** Before choosing a school, help your teen research:

✓ **Starting salaries in their field** – Is the degree cost justified by potential earnings?

✓ **Debt-to-income ratio** – Will they be able to **comfortably pay off student loans?**

✓ **Alternative paths** – Would **trade school, bootcamps, or employer training** lead to the same career at a lower cost?

◆ **Example:**

• A **student wants to study psychology** but isn't sure if grad school is financially realistic. Instead of jumping into loans, they **work in an entry-level counseling role first** to test the field before committing to more education.

◆ **Final Thought: College is a Tool, Not a Requirement**

✓ College is a great option for many careers — but it's not the only path.

✓ Choosing a financially smart way to attend matters just as much as choosing the right major.

✓ Your teen's success isn't defined by a degree — it's defined by how they build their skills, experience, and opportunities.

◆ **What's Next?**

Now that we've explored **the different paths after high school,** let's take a closer look at **how to ensure your teen makes a financially smart decision.**

◆ **Up Next: Encouraging Growth Without Pressure.**

📖 Section 8: Encouraging Growth Without Pressure

Once your teen has explored their **strengths, interests, and career options**, the next challenge is **helping them move forward without making them feel rushed or overwhelmed.**

Many parents worry:

✓ *How do I encourage my teen to take action without making them feel like I'm forcing a decision?*

✓ *What if they aren't making progress or keep changing their mind?*

✓ *How do I help them stay motivated without adding too much pressure?*

The key is **supporting their growth while giving them the space to make their own choices.** You want to help them take **small steps toward their future** while keeping the door open for **change and discovery.**

◆ The Balance Between Guidance and Independence

Your teen **still needs your support**, but they also need the **freedom to make their own decisions.** Here's how to **strike that balance.**

◆ 1. Be a Sounding Board, Not a Dictator

You want to help guide them, but **they need to feel ownership** over their future.

◆ Example Parent Dialogue:

✓ **Parent:** "I know this is a big decision, and I'm here to help you figure it out."

✓ **Teen:** "I just don't know where to start."

✓ **Parent:** "That's okay! Let's start small – what's one career or topic you'd like to learn more about?"

Why this works: It makes the conversation **collaborative** instead of feeling like an **interrogation.**

◆ 2. Celebrate Effort, Not Just Results

Progress isn't just about **choosing a career.** Even small steps – like researching a career, talking to a mentor, or taking a course – are **worth celebrating.**

Example Parent Dialogue:

✓ **Parent:** "I noticed you looked up information about cybersecurity. That's awesome! What stood out to you?"

✓ **Teen:** "I didn't realize there were so many jobs in the field."

✓ **Parent:** "That's great! Want to check out a beginner course or job shadow someone in the industry?"

Why this works: It **encourages curiosity** without making them feel like they need all the answers immediately.

3. Encourage Curiosity Over Commitment

If your teen feels **paralyzed by the pressure to make a decision,** remind them that they **don't have to lock into one career path today.**

Example Parent Dialogue:

✓ **Parent:** "Instead of picking a 'forever career,' what's something you'd like to explore right now?"

✓ **Teen:** "I like technology, but I'm not sure if I want to be a programmer."

✓ **Parent:** "That's okay! There are lots of careers in tech that don't require coding – let's see what else is out there."

Why this works: It **removes pressure** and shifts the focus to **exploration.**

* **Handling Setbacks, Indecision, and Self-Doubt**

Many teens **second-guess themselves** or feel stuck. Here's how to help them move forward.

1. Help Them Reframe Failure as Learning

Some teens **avoid making decisions** because they're afraid of **choosing wrong.** Teach them that failure is **part of the process.**

Example Parent Dialogue:

✓ **Teen:** "What if I pick the wrong career?"

✓ **Parent:** "That's completely normal! Most people try different things before they find the right fit. Every experience teaches you something useful."

Why this works: It **removes the fear of failure** and encourages them to **take action.**

2. Help Them See the Big Picture

Sometimes, teens feel like they **should have everything figured out already.** Remind them that **careers evolve over time.**

◆ **Example Parent Dialogue:**

✓ **Parent:** "Careers aren't set in stone. Most adults switch jobs multiple times. You're just starting out, so it's okay to change directions later!"

▨ *Why this works:* It **eases the pressure** to make a **"perfect" choice** right now.

◆ **3. Let Them Experience Small Risks**

Teens learn best **through experience.** Give them space to **test out careers without high stakes.**

◆ **Example Parent Dialogue:**

✓ **Parent:** "I know you're curious about video editing. Want to take on a small project for fun and see how you like it?"

▨ *Why this works:* It **encourages action** without making it feel like a **huge decision.**

* **Encouraging Growth Without Rushing**

Helping your teen move forward **doesn't mean rushing them into a decision.** It means **giving them opportunities to explore** while reminding them they're **in control of their own future.**

* **Final Parent Tips:**

  ✓ Encourage **curiosity, not commitment.**

  ✓ Support **small steps and celebrate progress.**

  ✓ Give them space to **explore without fear of failure.**

* **What's Next?**

You've guided your teen through **career exploration** and **decision-making.** Now, how do you continue to support them **without hovering?**

* **Up Next: Being Their Best Support System.**

📖 Section 9:
Being Their Best Support System

Your teen is **stepping into the next phase of their life,** and while they may not have everything figured out yet, they **don't have to navigate it alone.**

Your role is shifting – from **decision-maker to supporter, from guide to trusted advisor.**

The best way to continue helping them? **Be available, be encouraging, and trust that they will figure things out in their own time.**

◆ How to Support Without Hovering

It can be tempting to **keep checking in, offering suggestions, or worrying if they seem unsure.** But real growth happens when teens feel **trusted to make their own choices.**

Here's how to **stay involved without micromanaging.**

◆ 1. Let Them Take Ownership

Your teen needs to feel that **their career journey belongs to them,** not just something you're managing for them.

◆ Example Parent Dialogue:

✓ **Parent:** "What's one small step you want to take toward your career goals this month?"

✓ **Teen:** "I guess I could reach out to someone in the field."

✓ **Parent:** "That sounds great! Do you want any help figuring out how to approach them, or do you feel good handling it on your own?"

Why this works: It keeps **them in the driver's seat** while showing you're still there for support.

2. Offer Advice Only When Needed

Instead of jumping in with **solutions,** ask if they actually **want advice first.**

Example Parent Dialogue:

✓ **Parent:** "Are you looking for advice, or do you just want to talk it out?"

✓ **Teen:** "I think I just need to vent for a minute."

✓ **Parent:** "Got it – go ahead, I'm listening."

Why this works: It makes them feel **heard** without feeling like they're being **pushed toward a decision.**

3. Celebrate Their Wins – Big and Small

Even if they haven't **landed their dream job yet,** every step forward is progress. Recognizing their effort helps **boost confidence** and keeps them motivated.

◆ Example Parent Dialogue:

✓ **Parent:** "I saw you updated your resume – nice job! That's a big step."

✓ **Teen:** "Yeah, I finally got around to it."

✓ **Parent:** "That's awesome! It's one of those things that's easy to put off, but now you're ready when opportunities come up."

Why this works: It reinforces **progress over perfection.**

- **Keeping the Conversation Open**

Even as your teen becomes more independent, it's important to **keep communication flowing.** Here's how to check in without making it feel forced.

1. Make Career Talks a Natural Part of Everyday Life

Instead of **formal career check-ins**, weave career discussions into **casual moments.**

Example Parent Dialogue:

- ✓ **At dinner:** "I read about a woman who started her own business in her 20s – want to hear how she did it?"

- ✓ **On a drive:** "I heard a podcast about the future of jobs in tech – thought you might find it interesting."

- ✓ **Watching TV:** "That character's job is interesting. What do you think it would be like to do something like that?"

Why this works: It makes career talk feel **casual and ongoing,** not like a high-pressure conversation.

2. Encourage a Growth Mindset

Teens who think **career success happens overnight** can get discouraged **when things don't go perfectly.** Teach them that **growth takes time.**

Example Parent Dialogue:

- ✓ **Teen:** "I applied for an internship, but I didn't get it."

- ✓ **Parent:** "That's frustrating, but applying was a great step! Do you want to tweak your resume and try again somewhere else?"

Why this works: It helps them see setbacks as **learning opportunities, not failures.**

- **Letting Go: Trusting Their Path**

At some point, you have to **trust that they will figure things out.** Your guidance is **invaluable,** but ultimately, they have to **take ownership of their journey.**

Here's how to support them **without stepping in too much.**

1. Resist the Urge to Overcorrect

Your teen will make choices you **might not have made.** That's okay. Ask yourself:

- *Is this about my fears, or their journey?*

  √ Instead of **correcting them immediately,** ask **why they're drawn to that path.**

- **Example Parent Dialogue:**
  - √ **Parent:** "I noticed you're considering a career in video game development – what interests you about that field?"
  - √ **Teen:** "I love the creative side of designing worlds and characters."
  - √ **Parent:** "That's really cool! Have you looked into what skills you'd need to break into the industry?"

  Why this works: It **validates their interest** while guiding them to **think critically.**

✦ 2. Remember, Detours Are Normal

Most people don't have **a straight career path.** Remind your teen that **it's okay to change their mind.**

✦ Example Parent Dialogue:

✓ **Teen:** "I thought I wanted to be a teacher, but now I'm not sure."

✓ **Parent:** "That's totally normal! What parts of it do you like, and what parts make you hesitate?"

Why this works: It **helps them reflect** instead of feeling like they're failing.

✦ 3. Your Support Means More Than Your Approval

Your teen may not **follow the exact path you envisioned,** but knowing they have your **support and belief** will give them the confidence to move forward.

✦ Example Parent Dialogue:

✓ **Parent:** "No matter what you decide to do, I know you're going to find something that fits you."

Why this works: It reassures them that **your love and support aren't conditional on their career choices.**

✦ Final Thought: You're Doing Better Than You Think

If you've made it this far, you **care deeply about your teen's future.** That alone makes a huge difference.

Reminder for Parents:

✓ You don't need to have all the answers.

✓ Your teen doesn't need a perfect plan – just a willingness to explore.

✓ Your role is to provide support, guidance, and encouragement.

Key Takeaway: The most valuable thing you can give them **is your belief in their ability to find their way.**

What's Next?

Now that your teen is moving forward, how do you continue supporting them **without overstepping?**

Up Next: Conclusion – Trust the Process.

📖 Conclusion:
Trust the Process

Guiding your teen through career exploration **isn't about having all the answers** – it's about being a steady source of **support, encouragement, and perspective** as they figure things out for themselves.

If there's one thing to take away from this guide, it's this:

- ✓ **Your teen's journey will unfold in its own way and at its own pace.**

- ✓ **No career path is linear, and that's okay.**

- ✓ **Your role isn't to chart the entire course for them, but to walk beside them, offering guidance when they need it and space when they don't.**

- ◆ **Career Paths Are Not Straight Lines – And That's a Good Thing**

If you think about your own career journey, chances are it **wasn't a straight path from A to B.**

- ✓ You may have **changed jobs, industries, or even gone back to school** at some point.

- ✓ You may have discovered **unexpected opportunities** that shaped your future in ways you never anticipated.

- ✓ You may still be figuring out what you want to do – and that's okay!

The same will be true for your teen.

- ✉ **Key Takeaway:** Instead of worrying about whether they're making the **"right" decision**, trust that they will learn, grow, and adapt along the way.

◆ What If They Struggle or Change Their Mind?

It's **normal** for teens to start on one path and realize it's not quite right for them. This doesn't mean they **failed** – it means they're learning.

◆ Example:

✓ A teen who pursues **engineering** might later realize they prefer **teaching math.**

✓ A student who starts a **business degree** might find they love **graphic design and pivot into marketing.**

☑ How Parents Can Support Change:

✓ Remind them that **career shifts are normal** and not a sign of failure.

✓ Encourage them to **take the skills they've gained** and apply them to new opportunities.

✓ Help them see that **detours often lead to new strengths and discoveries.**

◆ Example Parent Dialogue:

✓ **Teen:** "I thought I wanted to do computer science, but I don't love coding."

✓ **Parent:** "That's completely okay! What parts of it did you enjoy? Maybe there's a career in tech that better fits your strengths."

☑ *Why this works:* It **keeps the conversation open** and reassures them that **exploring is part of the process.**

◆ Your Support Means More Than Your Advice

At the end of the day, **your teen's success won't come from you making the right decision for them – it will come from them learning to make decisions for themselves.**

318

What they need most from you **isn't a roadmap – it's belief in their ability to navigate the journey.**

✦ **The Most Valuable Things You Can Give Your Teen:**

✓ **Encouragement** – Let them know you believe in them, even if they're unsure of their path.

✓ **Patience** – Give them the space to explore and change directions if needed.

✓ **Perspective** – Remind them that success is about growth, not a perfect first decision.

▨ **Key Takeaway:** Your teen **will remember your support far more than any career advice you give.**

◆ **Actionable Next Steps for Parents**

Now that you've **helped your teen explore their future**, what can you do to keep supporting them **without overstepping?**

📌 **Here are three small but meaningful ways to stay involved:**

✓ **1. Check in occasionally – without pressure.**

> ◆ *Example:* "I know you were looking into psychology careers – have you learned anything interesting?"

✓ **2. Celebrate small wins.**

> ◆ Example: "I saw you signed up for that internship – that's awesome!"

✓ **3. Keep an open-door policy.**

> ◆ Example: "No matter what, I'm always here if you want to talk about what's next."

✅ *Why this works:* It **keeps communication open** without making them feel like they're being constantly evaluated.

◆ Final Thought: You're Doing Better Than You Think

By reading this book, you've shown that you **care deeply about your teen's future.** That alone makes a huge difference.

◆ Reminder for Parents:

✓ You don't need to have **all the answers.**

✓ Your teen doesn't need to make **a perfect choice today.**

✓ Your role is to **support, encourage, and trust that they will figure it out.**

Your belief in them **matters more than you realize.**

No matter where their journey takes them, they will **always have you in their corner.**

◆ **What's Next?**

There is no single **"right" path** for your teen – only the one that makes the most sense for them. **Trust their ability to figure it out.**

✓ **Keep the conversation open.**

✓ **Support their journey, even if it looks different from what you expected.**

✓ **Remember that careers evolve, and there's no single perfect choice.**

Your teen is **lucky to have your support.** Now, it's time to let them explore, grow, and discover their own path – knowing that you'll always be in their corner.

☑ **You've done your part. Now, trust the process.**

What's Next?

This book was written as a companion to *Can't I Just Stay in My Room?*, a teen career guide for kids who'd rather not talk about it. If your child is still figuring things out (or actively avoiding the conversation), that's the place to start.

If college isn't part of the plan – or your teen closed the first book and still didn't want a dorm room – there's a follow-up just for them:

Can't I Just Skip College?

For Everyone Who Closed the First Book and Still Didn't Want a Dorm Room

You can find both books, along with bonus materials, at https://cantijust.com.

——

For Educators and Counselors

If you work with students, we've created educator-friendly versions of our tools.

Downloadable PowerPoint slides, printable workbooks, and teacher guides are available to support classroom or group use. Visit our For Schools page at cantijust.com to learn more.

——

Be Part of the Mission

Wayfinder exists to help young people build better futures—with confidence, clarity, and a little less panic. If this book helped you support your teen, we'd love it if you left a review on Amazon or shared it with someone else who needs it.

You can also follow us online for updates, new books, free resources, and a little encouragement when the road ahead feels uncertain.

We're glad you're here.

About the Author

Jennifer Larsen has a habit of turning big questions into clear, doable steps—and she's built a career around helping others do the same. With a background in education and psychology (and a low tolerance for boring advice), she has created these guides for anyone tired of being asked, "What do you want to be when you grow up?"—especially if they're already grown.

Free Educator Toolkit

Want to bring these conversations into your classroom or office?

Scan the QR code to access the **Wayfinder Educational Toolkit** – a free companion to this book series designed for teachers, counselors, and support staff. You'll get:

- A **ready-to-use PowerPoint presentation** for classroom or group use

- A **printable workbook** with questions and activities for students or families

These tools are designed to make career and college planning easier for everyone – no training required.

Single-User License Granted

License for Supplemental Teaching Materials

The downloadable materials linked via this QR code – including PowerPoint presentations, student workbooks, and other teaching resources – are licensed for use **only** by the original purchaser of the book in which this QR code appears.

Permitted Use:

- You may download, reproduce, and use these materials in **any classes you personally teach**.

- You may share printed or digital copies with **your own students only**, as part of your instruction.

- You may store copies on your personal devices or educational platforms you manage for this purpose.

Prohibited Use:

- You may **not** share or redistribute this QR code, the download link, or the materials themselves with other educators, schools, or institutions.

- You may **not** upload the materials to public websites, shared drives, or repositories accessible by others.

- You may **not** resell or republish these materials in whole or in part.

This license relies on your integrity as an educator. If your colleagues would benefit from these materials, please encourage them to support the project by purchasing their own copy of the book.

Thank you for respecting the work that went into creating these resources.

The Can't I Just… Series
Real-world advice. Practical tools. No fluff.

Wayfinder's *Can't I Just…* series helps students, parents, and educators navigate the big transitions in life with clarity and confidence. Each title blends practical guidance with approachable activities so readers can turn ideas into action.

Other books in the series include:
• Can't I Just Stay in My Room? — A career guide for teens who aren't ready to "pick a major" yet.
• Can't I Just Skip College? — Exploring real-world options beyond a traditional degree.
• Can't I Just Help My Kid Pick A Path? — A parent's guide to supporting career exploration without pressure.
• Can't I Just Be Like Everyone Else? — A teen guide to soft skills, communication, and fitting in without faking it.

Visit CantiJust.com for resources, downloads, and the full book list.

About Wayfinder Foundation Inc.

Wayfinder Foundation Inc.

Wayfinder Foundation Inc. provides educational tools, resources, and programming to help youth and adults explore careers, build life skills, and improve emotional resilience.

Through book donations, school partnerships, and community programs, we aim to give every learner access to guidance that is practical, encouraging, and free from unnecessary barriers.

Learn more or get involved at:
WayfinderFoundationInc.org
Instagram & Facebook: @WayfinderFoundation